MW01380165

GETTING THERE
Frontier Travel
Without Power

GETTING THERE
Frontier Travel
Without Power

BY

SUZANNE HILTON

W

THE WESTMINSTER PRESS
Philadelphia

BOOK DESIGN BY DOROTHY ALDEN SMITH

First edition

Published by The Westminster Press ®
Philadelphia, Pennsylvania

PRINTED IN THE UNITED STATES OF AMERICA
9 8 7 6 5 4 3 2 1

Library of Congress Cataloging in Publication Data

Hilton, Suzanne.
  Getting there.

  Bibliography: p.
  Includes index.
  SUMMARY: Describes what it was like to travel by horseback, stagecoach, canalboat, flatboat, covered wagon, and sailing ship before the days of motorized travel.
  1. Transportation—United States—History—Juvenile literature. 2. Transportation—History—Juvenile literature. [1. Transportation—History] I. Title.
HE203.H48   380.5′0973   79-23196
ISBN 0-664-32657-9

PHOTOGRAPH CREDITS

The author is indebted for photographs in this book to:

Bancroft Library, University of California at Berkeley, p. 152.

Every Saturday, pp. 15, 33

Free Library of Philadelphia Photography Department, pp. 67, 137, 167

Harper's Bazaar, p. 59

Harper's Weekly, pp. 71, 110, 133, 135

Illustrated London News, p. 161

Library of Congress Photographic Library, pp. 17, 22, 23, 36, 54, 105, 113, 118, 120, 148, 173

National Archives Photo Library, pp. 58, 64, 65, 66, 127, 129

New York State Department of Transportation, p. 97

Harry L. Rinker, Delaware & Lehigh Canal Society, pp. 86, 89, 91, 124

State Archives of Pennsylvania, 83, 101

Three Tuns School, Ambler, Pa., p. 39

U.S. Department of the Interior, National Park Service, pp. 27, 45, 52, 53, 63, 80, 93, 95, 140, 141, 150

CONTENTS

PREVIEW

Not so long ago, the word "energy" applied to people power, not machine power.

Imagine taking long trips without airplanes, trains, buses, steamships, or the family automobile. In the early days when our country was being settled, the only energy burned on a long trip was the energy supplied by nature. Power came from wind, water currents, and four-footed animals. These three, combined with the endless energy of a human being who wanted to go somewhere, developed most of the United States before 1850.

What travelers our ancestors were! Put them in creaking ships on the sea and for months they survived wormy food, rationed water, and diseases. Point them toward the west and for weeks they walked, rode on animals, or tumbled about in wagons. Show them a river and they built boats to float downstream with the floods and to pole back upstream. Give them land where the rivers ran the wrong way and they built canals. Americans were determined to explore their big new country.

In two hundred years, travel changed very little. The only

improvement in horseback travel was a better brand of waterproof raincoat. Stagecoach travel improved when the Concord coach and macadamized roads were developed, so that even after automobiles were in use, people were still "staging it" in the mountains. Clipper ships shortened long sea voyages, but added little for the comfort of the passenger. With each improvement, Americans were able to travel a little farther west.

Steam engines did make a difference, though. On the rivers with flatboats were steamboats. Stagecoaches raced alongside steam railroad engines. But, for many thousands of travelers, engines were not to be trusted until after they had proven themselves. The people in the pages of this book traveled without engines and motors. To them, travel meant gritting the teeth, setting the chin, and bearing up without complaining.

Women and children traveled nearly as much as men, but almost never alone. They had no special comforts, although the men usually protected them from the worst conditions. Women and children were offered seats inside a stage on a rainy day or the first choice of beds in a tavern. These same men expected their women to be just as good cooks, housekeepers, and baby tenders on the prairie or at sea as they were at home. The kind of woman who fainted at the sight of a snake, panicked in a storm at sea, or could not handle a wagon and team of oxen in an emergency, did not travel very often.

Finding out how these early tourists felt is to discover something new about our ancestors. All the quotes in this book are the words of real persons, written as they were traveling—not years later.

Come along—taste the food, watch the expenses, feel the

suspicions toward strangers, discover odd local customs, move more slowly than you have ever traveled before. Feel the joy of journeying along with those survivors who were your ancestors. In these pages, enjoy adventures of the past. Then follow their lead and try the same kind of travel on your next vacation.

Ready to leave? There is no seat belt to buckle—you won't move faster than eight miles an hour. There are no fast-food places with twenty-eight flavors of ice cream, no motels with swimming pools along the highway. There aren't even any highways.

Happy journey!

1

SAILING ACROSS THE ATLANTIC

The Only Way to Come

"Infernal seasick," wrote Charles Leland in his diary.

He could hardly force himself to sit up and hold a pen. Leland was propped up on a narrow bunk that had a board along the side to keep him from rolling out onto the floor.

The whole cabin was no larger than the double bed he slept in back home. Luckily, Leland had to share the small space with only one other man, since he had the money for a cabin "above decks" on a first-class packet ship. Passengers who had to travel "between decks" were not so lucky.

Travelers to America, except those who were thrown into the holds of slave or prison ships, came to make a new life. Some, tired of wars at home, wanted to raise their children to know peace. Some had sons who could never own a piece of land in the old country. There just was not enough land to go around. In England, only the eldest son could inherit his father's land. Other travelers were just plain adventurers who wanted to see the New World. But for them all, there was only one way to get here—by sailing ship.

Sailing ships were not fast, because they depended on the wind. Unfortunately, the wind came most often from out of the west. To sail west against the wind, the ship had to zigzag, catching the wind first on one side of the sails, then on the other. To make matters worse, ships sailing west had to avoid getting into the Gulf Stream, which also flowed in the wrong direction for people who wanted to reach the New World. The shortest trip they could hope for was six weeks. They were happy to make it in eight.

The cheapest fare was 6 or 8 pounds sterling, or about $50, for each adult in the family. This expense was still too much for some families. One way to pay later was to sign on with the ship's captain and agree to be "indentured" as a servant to a person already living in America. That person then paid the passage and took home the immigrant and his family to work for him for several years.

Once a family made up their mind to leave the homeland, they packed their valuables and headed for the nearest seaport. There they waited until they could get passage on a ship sailing west across the Atlantic.

Packing to Go

Packing up valuables was often painful. So many things had to be left behind. What a family most valued in the old country was not necessarily going to be of value in the New World. Featherbeds inherited from parents couldn't be taken along. Instead, the family needed mattresses stuffed with straw or corn shucks, because these could be emptied and spread out to dry when the bedding got wet. Fashionable clothes were left behind and only clothes of tough, long-lasting materials were taken. Shoes and boots could not be bought cheaply in America, so trunks bulged with shoes, boots, and woolen coats.

Favorite toys were left behind to make room for cooking utensils and mechanics' tools. The family's best clothing was sealed inside a wooden box and sprinkled with camphor or tobacco to make it smell fresh. The oldest clothes were packed in canvas sacks to be handy for wear on shipboard. Fresh water was rationed carefully on the ship. Not one item of clothing could be washed except in seawater. Diapers washed out in this salty water never quite got dry, and

Leaving for America. While their parents have a last look at home, the children can hardly wait to board their ship

babies protested every day of the voyage. Men could not even shave until the last day at sea, when the captain finally allowed them to use the fresh water that was left in the scuttlebutt.

Getting the food ready for the eight-week trip kept the family kitchen busy for days. The women were responsible for feeding their own families. One woman from each family would be allowed her time at the shipboard stove, but it was best to have plenty of food prepared ahead of time.

The women boiled milk with sugar and poured it in little bottles. A bottle was sealed by knotting a string around the cork and around the neck, so no one could open it until ready to use, thereby ensuring that the milk would not sour during the long trip. They dipped baskets of potatoes into boiling water, dried out the potatoes in a hot oven, and packed them in sacks. They made yeast up into little cakes so they could bake bread on board ship, and they also prepared dried fish. All these foods kept well.

The women made many foods ahead of time—such as the children's favorite pudding of potatoes, bacon, and onion, covered with a crust. They made gingerbread and small cakes of flour and boiled potatoes. They packed molasses to sweeten their coffee and to use as medicine for the children. For extra treats they took dried fruits. For a special occasion at sea, the family cook used dried plums to make a duff—a sort of pudding of flour boiled with the dried fruit and topped with molasses.

With all their food and belongings packed high on a cart, the family arrived at a seaport town and found a room for the night. The next day, they set out to find the right ship to sail on. Advice came from all sides.

The Home at Sea

"Pick a ship with high bulwarks . . . then you won't get wet with every wave that comes over her side," said one friend.

"Look at the shape of her bottom," said another, "to see how fast she'll go through the waves. If she's too round, she'll probably bob up and down like a hobbyhorse when it gets rough."

Most travelers were not sure what to do with the advice

Shipbuilders tried different designs, but ships with high bulwarks were drier in stormy seas

they heard. Few had even seen a ship before. How round a bottom was too round? How high were waves at sea? What was the best time of year to sail?

The best advice, which all experienced travelers agreed on, was to sail with a captain who gave his passengers a contract. The contract told how much the trip would cost, when the ship would sail, and where it would land. Without a contract, passengers were at the mercy of a captain who could drop them anywhere he chose to go along the coast of the United States. Or a captain might charge money for dozens of little items—like sea biscuits—that were supposed to be free on shipboard.

Only the poorer passengers cooked their own food on the voyage. Charles Leland paid three times their low fare to travel first class. He could walk on the deck anytime he chose. At mealtime, he ate in a dining saloon where the dinner table and seats were screwed to the floor. The table had a little fence around it, like a billiard table, to catch sliding dishes. He ate buckwheat cakes, pastry, meat, and fresh poultry. After dinner, he and the other gentlemen went out on deck for cigars and jokes or sat around the table playing whist and casino. Leland knew he had chosen a good ship on his first day out. One of the crewmen told him that in port two cats had come on board voluntarily. They were still on the ship—a first-rate sign of a safe ship.

Travelers who went cheaply traveled "between decks." They did not even know how comfortable life could be "above decks." They were allowed to walk on a small portion of deck only a few hours during the day. But they were not concerned about comfort. They knew the voyage lasted only a few months. A man could be just as seasick above decks as between. All the passengers, rich or poor, would arrive in America on the same day. And the poor traveler had just as much chance to become a millionaire in the New World as the man who lounged in a comfortable saloon on the main deck.

Every traveler expected to make money in America. In the year 1845, an immigrant could earn $100 a year working as a hired hand on a farm. He could be happy with that money if he didn't "let a native whistle in his ear" and make him discontented. An artisan who was good with tools made more money in this new world than a schoolteacher, a clerk, or even a literary gentleman. Carpenters earned $1 a day— with free board!

A man could let his wife work and earn another $50 a year. His strong sons would make $4 a month hiring out for farm work. Even his daughters could get jobs doing housework. In the United States, working girls were not called "servants," but "helps." In some homes, the "helps" were even invited to sit down and eat with the family. With such dreams in their heads, poor families found it easy to live "between decks."

Cast Off

Early on the morning of sailing day, the "between decks" passengers jostled for a place in line on the wharf. Sailors shouted orders. Babies squalled. Mothers shrieked for missing children and missing children howled for their families. The emigrants carried cabbages, loaves of bread, cheese, butter, milk, beer, boxes, beds, bundles, and babies.

Finally the ropes let down the gangplank and the passengers clambered on board, hustling below to claim their berths. Berths were built along the sides and down the center of the ship. The choice ones were midships (where there was less rocking motion) and near the main hatchway (where there was fresh air occasionally). Men took the top berths, women the lower. As soon as a family claimed their spot, they tacked their names over the bunks. Then they hung curtains around them by attaching sheets to the wooden beams above. This gave each family a tiny "cabin" to call their own. It also was a constant fire hazard.

Each family brought one large, tough, deal chest, bound at the corners with iron. Inside it were the family treasures —father's tools, the family Bible, mother's teapot, boots, and heavy coats. Nothing in this chest was used during the whole voyage, because it was nailed shut and sealed with a lock. As soon as the family chose their berths, this chest was bolted to the ship's floor with cleats and became the family dining table.

The last few hours before the ship sailed, the deck was cluttered with bodies—all kneeling, crouching, lying, squatting, or sitting as each wrote a last letter to send ashore to loved ones.

The actual time of sailing depended on the tide and the wind. When the wind came from the wrong direction, the ship was towed to a starting point. Then the decks were cleared for the sailors. Everyone looked forward to the next day "when we shall shake down and get our sea legs." Usually the passengers were disappointed to find that it took longer than a day to get used to life on a rolling ship.

Between decks, families busily unpacked cooking utensils to make the first meal. A steward told each cook what time she was allowed to use the tiny stove. Bowls were made of wood, forks and spoons were of iron, and the one family drinking cup was of tin. Only the glass bottles of milk were breakable. A guidebook had told each family what to bring:

one small frying pan	a wooden tub filled with
a cooking kettle	salted beef
tin pot to hang in	a lantern and a can of lamp
front of fire	oil
one teapot	Epsom salts
a tin bowl with	bilious pills
handle	magnesia and castor oil
one small baking pan	a tin to keep bread in
for bread	a can for fresh water

Each morning a ship's officer rationed out the fresh water. If it was spilled, there was no more until the next day. Each family kept its water in a tin can.

For seasickness, the cooks made a watery porridge, or people drank barley water and diluted vinegar. Above decks, the first-class passengers tried sucking lemon drops, smoked cigars, and ate baskets of fresh fruits. Nothing really worked. The seasickness disappeared by itself in a few days.

Life at Sea

Most passengers wondered why sailors were not totally confused by the mass of ropes on a sailing ship. But within a week, the passengers were so accustomed to the various sounds on the decks above them that when they heard certain orders, they knew just how to brace themselves. The different sea chanteys the sailors sang to time their movements while they weighed anchor, hoisted sail, and pulled on halyards became as familiar as lullabys.

"A boat is not such a bad place after all," Leland decided once he got his sea legs. He and his friends played "shovelboard," formed musical groups, watched porpoises, lay on the lifeboats in the sun, and sometimes just looked down at the steerage passengers as they walked, cooked, and ate on the deck in nice weather.

Some days at sea there was no wind at all. Then the ship lurched up and down, the sails flapping uselessly. The passengers made a game of "whistling up a wind" for the captain. Sailors were superstitious about whistling. They permitted it only during dead calms.

Other days, the travelers below heard the zinging of the salt water as the waves smacked hard against the ship's hull. They were all lighthearted then because they were moving west.

Packets such as the *Morning Star* were fast, but wet on deck

This newspaper picture of the brig *Somers* frightened travelers in 1847

"Went on deck," said Charles Leland, "rolling and tumbling gloriously, a spanking breeze from the east northeast . . . the ship tearing and smashing along like a hurricane, leaning over all on one side . . . hard work dressing . . . the basin leaned over so much I could hardly get in enough water . . . ca-smash! Half the crockery seems to have fallen off the dinner table . . . an unfortunate lurch broke tumblers, upset a pitcher, and spilt sugar."

Down below, the travelers in the cheaper berths were not so jubilant. Pots and pans skittered across the floor. Babies shrieked in terror. Several families spilled their water rations for the day. One lady said she could not get her clothes on because she had to hold on to a post.

"Sometimes I forget for a moment and let go . . . then away I go . . . bumped into Mrs. Reed, who fell full tilt against her looking glass and broke it to atoms."

Excitement at sea came rarely—except for the occasional

storms that no one really hoped to see. Sometimes large fish
—a swordfish or a dolphin—scared up a school of flying fish
that landed on the deck. The high point of each day for
first-class passengers came at noon when the captain took his
observations and marked the distance they had traveled on
the chart. Some even doubted the captain's calculations and
measured the distance on the chart themselves, using a
piece of pocket string or the edge of a handkerchief to see
how far they had moved since noon of the day before.

Betting was the number one occupation. Passengers bet
each other how far they would travel each day or bet which
day they would see a sail—any excuse would do for a bet. On
his first trip to America, the British stage actor Tyrone
Power told about betting on a white sail ahead.

"We were rapidly approaching," said Power, "although a
stern chase is usually a long chase."

"It must be the *Tallahassee,* Captain Glover," announced
a passenger. The *Tallahassee* had left port just ahead of their
ship with Captain Glover as master. As they drew nearer,
the odds rose in favor of the ship being the *Tallahassee.* It
had a flush deck like hers. Also, it was a tall, long ship and
square built. So was this one. It had stump royal masts and
a storm house abaft, too.

"The nearer we came," Power said, "the less ardour
amongst the backers of the *Tallahassee.*"

The two ships ran closer to each other, and the backers
were silent. Everyone ran forward to the forecastle to have
a better look, except Power and a few friends. A straggler
came back toward them with a sneaking offer to hedge the
bet. He had no takers. Gradually, the other passengers
filtered back, making remarks about the ship that was no
longer so far ahead.

"It can't be the *Tallahassee*, because she has copper trim." "She had a white line over her side." "She could not be sailing so slowly."

"Trifles like this," said Power, "were all-sufficient occupation for the day. They served as subjects of conversation for hours after."

The greatest event in crossing the ocean was when another sail came in sight and then that ship came close enough to "speak." The first question was always, "Where are you bound?" followed closely by, "Where are you from?" and "Is there any news?" The captains of the two ships exchanged the latest news each had heard before sailing. That way the small group of passengers in the middle of the ocean were the first to hear of any important news affecting either side of the Atlantic. But for the passengers of both ships, the happiest result of speaking another ship was when the ships reached port. Then each captain reported having seen the other ship safe and on its course. This news was immediately published in the newspaper, and those left back home knew that the ship carrying their loved ones had been seen.

With the latest news on their tongues, the outbound travelers no longer felt so alone in the world. They had a tie with the shore that they were fast approaching.

Toward the end of the voyage, the between-decks people began comparing notes on the new life ahead for them. A few lucky ones had relatives in the New World whose letters told them what to expect. They shared the information they had and also shared a good many rumors and half-truths. But emigrants who left the old country after 1848 had a new book, printed in England, which was filled with useful information. *Hints to Emigrants, or to Those Who May Contem-*

plate Emigrating to the U.S.A. was shared by everyone between decks.

According to *Hints to Emigrants,* two families of four persons each, with assorted small children, could begin life very well for 63 pounds sterling (or $321 for the first year), if they went to farming. The book advised them first to buy already cleared land—somewhere between 37° and 41° latitude, where it was neither too hot nor too cold.

Cleared land was the cheapest to buy, because having it cleared cost $4 an acre. However, there was an advantage to buying forested land because a good woodsman could cut trees down for 50 cents a day and the emigrant could build a home with the logs. The cost of land was rising fast. A man could buy forty acres for $400 in 1802. But in only two years, that price had risen ten times.

Men who came from countries where trees had long ago been called an endangered species could not imagine owning trees that could be cut down. They were shocked to read that oak trees were cut down in the New World to make fence rails. In the old country, oak trees were saved to make the most expensive furniture for royalty. Men were surprised to learn they could build a shanty frame house, a stable, and outbuildings for as little as $50. The same buildings would have cost them over ten times as much back home. Surely they were headed for a land of great wealth!

The emigrants' book said that one man and a stout (meaning strong, not fat) boy could prepare five or six acres the

The *Emigrant's Guide* warned travelers to leave the crowded seaport cities and head for country

first winter. A first crop of Indian corn and potatoes could be followed by wheat, if the land was good. The family must buy many provisions for their first winter, but a small garden would give them all the vegetables they would need. One horse and three cows would produce enough manure to fertilize the garden, and the cows would supply milk for the family.

In the New World, stock animals lived outdoors because there was so much space. They ate less, too, than animals kept in barns. Cows roamed in the woods and found their own food. In winter, the emigrants cut up hay, straw, and corn stalks, mixed them with boiling water, and sprinkled in bran or cornmeal to feed the cows. As the men talked about the farms they would own someday, they all realized that this was only their first trip. Soon, they would all travel far from the cities to find these wonderful, cheap farms.

"Land Ho!"

Suddenly one morning, shipboard passengers awoke to hear strange scratching sounds on the deck. The sailors were cleaning the decks with holystones and sand. Other sailors began painting the ship's woodwork and varnishing every inch of mahogany. This was a sure sign that land was near. Ships always entered a seaport looking as if they had had the quietest kind of voyage. It was good publicity for the ship and its owners.

The cry of "Land ho!" only verified what the passengers had already suspected. Between-decks passengers rushed to look out of the tiny portholes. The few who made it to the top of the hatchway reported to those below. There was nothing to be seen but water. The only person on the ship who saw land was the lone sailor atop the highest mast.

The cry suddenly lifted any gloom that lurked below. The emigrants had made it! The last bet was made—on what day and what time the ship would drop anchor or touch a wharf. But this bet was only halfhearted. There was suddenly too much to do. By the time the ship entered the harbor, all the travelers were taking their first baths since leaving home, using the last of the fresh water, which no longer had to be saved for emergencies. The men shaved. Children were scrubbed until they yelled for pity.

Everyone peeled off the filthy clothes worn for the past two months and tossed them overboard. They emptied the straw from all the mattress covers and with it went most of the bedbugs and lice. The sea behind the ship was floating with debris. Then each family opened the wooden box and an aroma of camphor or tobacco escaped. Every passenger dressed in Sunday-best clothes. At last they were ready to greet the United States health officer.

They were no longer "emigrants" now. As they entered the New World, they were called "immigrants." They held hands tightly in family groups as they left the ship. This was the place where the emigrants' book had told them to worry about sharks—land sharks. Well-dressed men were not necessarily gentlemen and honorable, the book warned. The new immigrants had to be careful about anyone trying to take their money. They turned in their foreign money for American dollars and, in 1848, received $4.44 for each pound sterling. They took steps to become naturalized at once. And, obedient to the last warning in the book, they planned to get out of the port city as quickly as possible. Their travels had just begun.

Strange Shores

Ahead of the new immigrants were discoveries of all kinds. Americans did not have fences and hedges growing around the edges of their property as Europeans had. New Englanders built their houses of wood and used their stones to build fences. Any right-thinking European knew that houses should be of stone and fences of wood. Beds in American taverns did not have curtains around them for privacy. And every American porch seemed to have a rocking chair. Were there really so many grandmothers in America, or did all Americans have spare time to sit down and rock? English travelers were envious of Americans who could make their own candles. In England, they had not been allowed to, even when they had their own sheep tallow. The hardest new custom to accept was the ever-present stove in American homes and taverns. The newcomers were used to cold rooms and they found the heat stifling.

But it was the people of the New World that surprised the newcomers the most—no matter how poor or ignorant an American might be, he could not be ordered about. Wealthy travelers had much trouble learning that even the people who served them had to be treated politely.

"You must treat Americans as all equals in the eyes of God," said an early travel book. The long voyage was over, but the education was only beginning.

2

RIDING WEST ON HORSEBACK

Shanks' Mare

One of the first surprises for newcomers was that Americans hardly ever walked. They called walking "going by shanks' mare" or "hoofing it," but from the very start of cross-country travel, America was too big for walking.

"Horseflesh is so plentiful that no one walks—except a tramp or a fool," people in the New World said. And an Englishman said, "No matter how poor or friendless, the American will somehow find a way to ride."

When an occasional walker took himself on "a pedestrian journey," no one respected him for it. An English traveler tried it once in 1800. He stopped at an inn in Lancaster, Pennsylvania, and asked for a cup of tea.

"No tea until suppertime," said the innkeeper's wife sternly.

"But I can't stay until then," protested the thirsty traveler. "I have many miles to walk before nightfall."

"No tea," said the woman, and shut the door.

A few years later, the same man happened to return to the

same inn. This time when he asked for a cup of tea, it was brought immediately. The difference, he was certain, was that the second time he was riding and the innkeeper's wife considered him a gentleman.

The Simplest Way

The cheapest way for a man to travel was to buy a horse. But Thomas Richards did not fancy himself on the back of a mare. He was a young teen-ager the summer of 1810 when he rode west to explore Ohio and Pennsylvania. Thomas owned a sulky that had impressed many of the young ladies in his town. He harnessed his mare to it, tied a wooden case of clothing on to the back, and got in.

Thomas was only twenty miles out of town when he discovered how bad the roads were. By the time he reached the foot of the first mountain ridge in Pennsylvania, the road was nothing but a rocky stream bed. The sulky was lightweight, and as it bounded from rock to rock the horse felt it shaking and bucking. At the top of a short hill, Thomas' mare took fright and bolted. The sulky followed, more often in the air than on the ground. Thomas hung on as long as he could.

"My horse overset my sulky and drawed me ten yards . . . head downwards," he said later. "I thought I was gone for sure."

Somehow he managed to disentangle himself from the reins and drop off onto the road. He struggled up the hill after his horse, picking up pieces of clothing that had fallen out of the broken case. Three miles farther along he found his horse still attached to the sulky. At least most of the sulky

The quickest way to travel was on horseback

pieces were there. In the next town, he sold the pieces and rode the rest of the way on horseback.

Traveling on horseback was fast. With a good horse, a rider averaged thirty miles a day. If he did not want to travel alone, he joined company for the day with other single riders along the way. The common greeting was "How do ye?" Said quickly, the phrase soon became just "Howdy." Back home, a formal introduction would have been necessary. But the traveling person did not have to worry about his friends seeing him talk to someone on a lower social level than his own. Sometimes the traveler even discovered that he enjoyed meeting and talking with strangers.

Buying a Mount

A good horse cost from $50 to $100—and a saddle was another $9. The price depended on what kind of horse it was and where it was bought. It also depended on how desperate the buyer was for a horse, because the seller asked as much money as he dared.

In the east, a buyer could not find a better horse than the Narragansett Pacer, bred in Rhode Island. This horse was sure-footed and had a broad back. But what riders liked best about the Narragansett Pacer was his gait—a curious sort of rocking motion that was very comfortable on long rides.

In the south, the rider looked for a Tennessee or Chickasaw horse. In the far west, however, a man riding a "states" horse was at a disadvantage. He would do well there to sell his "states" horse and buy an Indian pony, a bronco, or another "California half-breed" horse. Western-bred horses were good at mountain climbing, fording swift streams, and living off the grasses found in the country.

A person with less money could buy a mule for travel in the west. But mules were stubborn and not even a pair of spurs made a mule go anyplace it did not want to go. A mule would not follow a strange trail unless it was led by another animal that the mule trusted. After several days of riding on a mule, one man said, "No other experience in life exactly fits you for riding a mule."

Camels first arrived in the American west in 1856. For a few years, travelers thought they had found the ideal mount for travel across desert country. A camel covered over 65 miles in a day. It carried its own water and seemed perfectly content to eat the ugliest bushes in the desert which no other animal would touch. But camels had bad tempers. They made horses and cattle stampede and so were not welcome in wagon trains. Besides, few men could ride a camel without getting seasick. So for most travelers, a horse was the best buy.

"Never buy a dish-faced horse," warned a traveler's guidebook. "They are not safe and have too much go-ahead in them."

The book also warned buyers that large, overgrown horses tired too quickly. Black horses could not stand the heat and white horses could not stand cold weather. A deep-bay horse with no white hairs would turn out to be a fool. Yet it would have great courage and independence, such as an army man might want.

The horse that a traveler wanted to buy was one of a light sorrel or chestnut color—providing it had some white hair. The more white hair it had on the feet, legs, and face, the kinder the horse would be. A horse that was broad and full between the eyes had good sense. It could be trained to do anything, but it would not stand for a whip.

The age of a horse was very important for the traveler who hoped to make his whole trip on the same animal. To find out how old a horse was, the buyer looked at the teeth. If the horse had shed the two corner teeth and his foreteeth, he was past four years. Between four and five, he cut the under tusks. His upper tusks were cut at five years and then his mouth was complete. At six years, the grooves and hollows in the teeth began to disappear as the teeth wore down. By seven years, they were fairly smooth, except for the corner teeth. When all the hollows and grooves were gone, the horse was past eight years and too ancient for a long trip.

Horse sellers drove a hard bargain. Often the buyer

needed a horse or he could not complete his trip and get home again. On the last day of June, one English traveler lost his horse when he was several miles from a city or a stagecoach road. He had no choice but to buy another horse. When he finally found one, the horse cost $100 and looked half blind.

"Yes, I know," said the seller agreeably. "But if he goes blind before Christmas, I'll give you $25 back." By that time, the traveler knew, he would be home in England.

On the Road

Travelers were on the road all seasons of the year. In the winter, the horseback rider had to roughen the horse's shoes

Almost every village had its blacksmith shop

so the animal would not slip on ice. In certain kinds of snow, its feet became "snowballed." The snow stuck like ice balls in the tender part of the hoof. When the horse limped, the rider had to dismount, clear out the ice balls, and then walk. Later, he took a piece of shoe leather and nailed it under the horse's shoe.

Horseback travelers often formed a company to journey together when the snow was deep. A horse could push through dry snow up to 2½ feet deep, but not for long. In a company, each rider took his turn riding in the lead to open up a track through the snow. Sometimes the riders themselves had to crawl on their hands and knees in front of the horses to open a track.

Almost every village had a blacksmith shop, so changing a horse's shoes was not a problem. But it was expensive. Shoes cost from 25 cents to 75 cents each, and some blacksmiths charged as much as 50 cents extra to remove old shoes.

A horse could live on water alone for as long as twenty-five days. But it could live only five days with food and no water. A horse that had been without water three days could drink over a hundred pounds of water at one time. The greatest danger of travel in the west was that a horse might drink alkali water or eat the grass around an alkali stream. Either meant death for the horse.

Riders were careful to let their horses drink before fording a stream. Otherwise, they might stop and try to drink in midstream, risking losing their footing or sinking down in quicksand. To swim a horse across a deep river, the rider dismounted. He grabbed the horse's tail in one hand, and in the other he held a rope attached to the bridle. With the rope, he kept the horse from turning back. By holding the tail, he kept himself from sinking.

Mosquitoes and horseflies—some as large as wasps—were everywhere, making life miserable for horse as well as rider. The horseflies were especially bad in the south, depositing eggs in sores on a horse's body. Treatment for sores along the road included tying a piece of bacon rind on the flesh while the horse was hot.

Northern horses ate oats. But horses in the south were corn-fed. As soon as a traveler arrived at an inn that served cornbread for dinner, he knew he had a problem. Out in the barn, his horse was being fed corn, too. When a grain-fed horse was given corn, it became so sick it could not travel. The same happened to a corn-fed horse when it was given grain. In large packtrains where there were many horses this problem was solved by carrying the horses' feed along. But this was not practical for the single traveler. Some tried, by hiring a local man to ride with them just to carry the horse's feed. Other travelers sold the grain-fed horse and bought a corn-fed horse so they could travel in the south.

Sleeping Places

East of the Mississippi River, horseback travelers usually had no trouble finding an inn for the night and a meal for 25 cents. Once in a long while, however, a rider found an inn where there was entertainment—at a high price. In a tiny Indiana village, William Cobbett found an inn that charged him $3 for the night in 1818—more than a New York hotel.

Horseback travelers had an advantage over stagecoach passengers. They did not have to stay at a stagecoach tavern, but could sleep at a cheaper inn or even in a private home. A man traveling alone was often invited to eat and sleep by a family's fireplace. He repaid their kindness by telling them about his adventures on the road. From some of these fireside visits came the rumor that all travelers were liars. Liar or not, a traveler usually gave a lonesome backwoods family an evening to be remembered.

Every inn had bedbugs. Tavern owners did not even try to get rid of them—they were a fact of life. A traveler who slept in a private home might have a night without bugs. Many people had made their beds of sassafras wood and put chips of the same wood into their drawers to keep bedbugs away.

Thomas Richards, who had started his trip in a sulky and ended up on horseback, was not worried about bedbugs

Many stagecoach taverns, like this one in Pennsylvania, saw more than 150 years of travelers come and go

when he stopped one summer evening at a tavern in Ohio. Reed's Tavern had several windows, so that he would get fresh air as well as have an escape in case of fire. Thomas did notice that only one of the windows could be opened, but it was growing dark and he had heard tales about thieves on the road. So he went in.

"Dark come and there was no candles," Richards said. "They gave me supper in the dark. While at supper, in come my noble landlord with eight drunken Irishmen. They behaved quiet till I got to bed. I was shown upstairs in the dark and found it was all in one room unfinished. My bed was immediately opposite one of the windows. Poor indeed. A thunderstorm come up. I hung up my greatcoat before the window. The wind blowed it down. The rain beat in. It was dreadful."

Then the men downstairs began getting louder.

"I laid still in dread. Placed my Pocket Book underneath me. Was alarmed at my situation, but bore it patiently. Presently, up comes one of the Irishmen, drunk, and tumbles on top of me. I got him off and out of the bed. And then come two more. Very much alarmed was I. Got up and was determined to call the landlord and not sleep there. Hunted about in the dark for the stairway when I heard a whispering with the infernal devils that they would 'be at them before morning.' I was frightened beyond all expression. My hair raised on my head. I found the stairs and took one or two steps and brought the floor below. Called up my noble landlord and noble lady and made them let me sleep in their room."

Before daybreak, Thomas went out to the barn for his horse and galloped as hard as he could back in the direction he had come from. He had seen all he wanted to see of Ohio.

Many times travelers had to spend the night outdoors rolled up in a blanket. They built a fire for warmth and to keep away wild animals. Even in the summer, nights in the mountains were cold. One snowy night, James Kenney found a hollow stump of a dead tree on one side of Allegheny Mountain. He scooped out the snow from the stump, made a floor of bark, and slept comfortably.

When the horseback traveler slept outdoors, he let his horse loose to roam and nibble grass. He learned quickly to attach a bell to the horse to help him find it in the morning. A thirty-foot length of rope trailed from the bridle to help him catch his horse.

Saddlebag Suitcase

With so little space to carry extra equipment, the traveler wore most of his clothing. He tied some around his saddle and stuffed the rest into a saddlebag. When the day was hot, he could ride along in his shirt sleeves. But when he came near a village, he put on his coat and hat to look presentable. To ride without any shirt at all was unthinkable—only savages did that!

Even in summer, nights could be cold. So the traveler also wore woolen stockings, winter underwear, and a dark wool shirt. He wore the same shirt for weeks without washing it, because he thought that since he wore an undershirt, the wool shirt did not come into contact with his body, so it never got dirty. Perhaps the resulting smell was blamed on his horse. He wore thick pantaloons as padding against the horse and saddle, high riding boots, a heavy sack coat, and an old hat that was soft enough to be used for a nightcap. A strap around his waist held everything together and supported his revolver plus a tin cup for drinking.

Around his saddle he packed a rolled-up greatcoat (a heavy overcoat with a cape over the shoulders), an extra set of underwear, a towel, a pair of old shoes, and a rubberized cloth for rainwear. Under the saddle, next to the horse's back, was the blanket he used for a bed.

The saddlebag held a tin box full of gingerbread or johnnycake (it was really called "journeycake") and another tin filled with lumps of "portable soup." Portable soup had been dried but with the addition of hot water made excellent soup. Another tin box held a mixture of linseed oil, turpentine oil, yellow wax, and tar. The traveler warmed this mixture in the hot sun or in front of a fire and rubbed it into his shoes or boots to make them waterproof. An extra sack held a coffeepot and a frying pan—both of them covered with soot from previous outdoor fires. The traveler never washed off the soot, because the black made the metal heat up faster. With a sack of flour and a side of bacon, he was ready for three weeks of independence on the road.

Fresh Food

The traveler used his gun to stretch out his food supply. The best gun he could find in 1855 was a single-barreled muzzle-loader for which he made his own bullets. He carried the gunpowder in a cow's horn that he had scraped smooth and thin with a piece of broken glass. The horn hung from one shoulder and just fit the curve of his body comfortably. When he spotted something he wanted for dinner, however, he could not just aim and fire.

First he sprinkled about a tablespoon of the black powder

from the small end of the cow's horn into his gun. Then he wadded in a greasy rag and rammed it down tight with a rod which was kept attached to his gun. Next he put in one of his homemade lead balls and pushed it tight against the rag. After that, he pushed down another rag to hold the bullet in tight. He aimed a little above his target's head and fired. If he missed, no animal ever gave him a second chance. He collected his greasy rags—and even the bullet if he could find it—to use the next time.

Not every traveler was as well armed. When Mark Twain went west in 1861, he told about his firearm.

"I was armed to the teeth with a pitiful little Smith & Wesson's seven-shooter which carried a ball like a homeopathic pill. It took the whole seven to make a dose for an adult. It only had one fault—you could not hit anything with it. One of our conductors on the stagecoach practiced awhile on a cow with it and, as long as she stood still and behaved herself, she was safe. But as soon as she went to moving about, and he got to shooting at other things, she came to grief."

George Bemis, who traveled with Mark Twain, had an Allen—a gun that most people called a "pepperbox."

"To aim along the turning barrel and hit the thing aimed at was a feat which was probably never done with an Allen in the world," said Twain. "But George's was a reliable weapon, nevertheless, because as one of the stage drivers afterward said, 'If she didn't get what she went after, she would fetch something else.' And so she did. She went after a deuce of spades nailed against a tree once and fetched a mule standing about thirty yards to the left of it. Bemis did not want the mule, but the owner came out with a double-barreled shotgun and persuaded him to buy it anyhow."

Weather-Wise

A horseback traveler had to learn to forecast the weather better than travelers who rode inside something covered. He kept a close watch and tried to memorize the thousands of hints that nature gave him. He knew it would be fair the next day if the sky was red at sunset . . . or if there was dew on the grass after a fair day . . . or if the summer evening was bright without falling stars . . . or if fields were covered with mist before sunrise . . . or if there was lightning without thunder after a clear day.

Bad weather was on the way when smoke blew down through the chimney . . . when old people complained about their corns and aches . . . when the moon had a halo . . . when no dew lay on the grass after a fair day . . . when the sky was red in the morning . . . when the sun's rays looked like Moses' horns . . . or when the sun set behind a bank of clouds on the horizon.

There were countless insect and animal signs to watch for. Before a fair day gnats swarmed at sunset, bats fluttered more, and beetles flew about. When sheep or goats fought more than usual, marigolds and chickweed closed their blossoms, cats washed their faces often, foxes and dogs howled, or pigs grunted loudly, the weather would be bad. Then one saw horses stretching out their necks, sniffing the air, and gathering in a corner of a field, their heads turned away from the wind.

The spider was one of the best weather predictors of all. It changed its web about every twenty-four hours. When it spun a web with long terminating filaments (the part that holds the web to something solid), the traveler could plan on

Daniel Boone views Cumberland Gap—one of the main trails west

The same place where Boone was standing as it looks today

ten fair days. The earlier in the morning the spider started work, and the more active it was, the finer the weather would be. If it was still changing its web between six and seven in the night, or if it was working during a rain, the next day would be fair.

Horse Sense

Every horseback traveler was his own horse doctor. Along the route, he could obtain molasses and new milk, as well as sage to make sage tea. He could find cedar, hemlock, oyster shells, wood ashes, white-ash bark, and beef bones, all of which could be made into medicines. When his horse had sores, he stopped at a house along the road and borrowed some used dishwater to wash them out.

A horse with a broken leg was too valuable to shoot. The owner strung it up with a sling to a barn rafter and cared for it until the break healed. For a traveler, the long healing period meant the end of a trip. He had no choice but to find a farmer who would take his injured horse as a gift. If there was no one around, then he had to shoot the animal.

One of the most serious problems a traveler on horseback had to deal with was the heaves. Horses usually got the heaves (difficulty with breathing) and foundered (became lame) when they had to eat a food they were not used to eating. A medical book on horses was not very encouraging when this happened on a trip. There were cures that might work for a horse that was at home and could be put back on its regular food. But, said the book, "broken-winded horses might as well be knocked in the head as to attempt to travel with them."

Horseback travelers had only homemade maps
to show them how to go through Cumberland
Gap into bluegrass country

Maps and Trails

Riding a horse was the ideal way to travel for a person who
had a streak of the explorer spirit. He did not have to stay
on a road, but might follow an Indian path that was often a
good shortcut. He could travel along creek bottoms where
he could find good grass and water for his horse.

Today's road maps show rivers and streams in very pale
ink, because with bridges and modern ways of traveling,
these wet and swampy places no longer affect the route. But
the map that early travelers looked at showed not only every
stream and creek along the path but also where they could
be forded, where the inns were, where the rider could find
wells with drinking water, and where the blacksmith shops
were.

Before leaving home, the traveler copied a map for himself—if he was lucky enough to see one. He also visited his friends and they told him where people they knew lived along his route. It never hurt to have friends in strange places, but it was no guarantee of future comforts either.

Joseph Paul had a long list in the back of his diary of places where he had been told to stop. Beside each name, he had written some hints for himself. There was "Roush, whose son keeps a tavern in Buffalo Valley" and "Maxwell in Somerset who is sick" and "the Silks who keep a public house at Bear Creek Saw Mill." Beside the Silks name, Joseph had later scratched the notation that their cows had been gone for two weeks and so there was no milk or cream for the coffee or butter for the bread. Their hens all had baby chicks, so there were no eggs either.

Many a road was no more than a track with marks blazed on the trees. William Cobbett found himself on such a road looking for a village in Indiana one day in 1818. A guide took him to the start of the trail, where slips of bark had been stripped off the trees every forty yards or so. The guide turned back, telling Cobbett that he "could not possibly make a mistake and get lost." But soon the blaze marks disappeared altogether and Cobbett was lost in the middle of the day with no compass. In such a fix, travelers had no choice but to keep wandering until something or someone set them back on the road.

Language Problems

One of the surprises of travel was discovering differences in the English language—all within the same United States. New Englanders had a habit of saying "I guess," while New

Yorkers sprinkled their talk with "I suspect," Pennsylvanians said "I expect," and Virginians used "I reckon."

"I expect you're going to 'Hio," a man said to teen-ager Margaret Van Horn one day in 1810. She had never heard of Ohio then and thought she was headed for New Connecticut, the name most New Englanders used for the western country.

The term "Yankee" referred only to a person who lived in upper New England, but as far west as Ohio anyone living north of New York City was a "Yankee." In England, even a person from Georgia was called a "Yankee." No one is certain where the word came from, but James Fenimore Cooper thought it came from the word "Yengeese," the Indian's way of saying "English."

Differences in language did not make it any easier to find the way to strange places, as Francis Parkman found out when he asked a farmer, "How far is it to Alton Bay?"

"Two mile strong," said the farmer.

"Two miles *what?*" asked Parkman.

"Two mile strong," repeated the farmer. "Rather more nor two mile."

Charles Dickens, visiting from England, could not understand the word "fixings" when a fellow diner urged him to "try some of these fixings." Dickens said that when an American was dressing, he was "fixing himself." When the tavernkeeper was getting ready for dinner, he was "fixing the tables." "Fixing food" meant cooking. The doctor "fixes" a person who is ill. The porter "fixes" the luggage.

Language in the far west was strange to all travelers. There the people were always saying "You bet" instead of "yes." "Go" became "get up and get." A nicely dressed woman "ragged out," and a loafer was a "bummer." "Bull-whacking" meant driving an ox team and a "biled shirt" was a white shirt. "Square" meant anything perfect or excellent, which is what a square meal originally meant. "How" spoken by an Indian was not supposed to be funny, but meant "How do you do?"

Money Problems

Language was not the only difference. A paper dollar, cut carefully into quarters, was called "cut money." It was common currency in Kentucky and Tennessee and the quarters were valued at 25 cents apiece. But the traveler who tried to use cut money in another state had problems.

Taylor Edward and a friend stayed in a small western Ohio town one night in 1816. When they paid their tavern bill the next morning with United States notes, they ran into a stubborn innkeeper.

"But paper money is legal," Edward told the man.

"I take only hard money here," the innkeeper insisted.

Edward argued and said that coins were too heavy to carry, especially when traveling on horseback. The new paper money was lightweight. Besides, since the War of 1812 had ended, coin payments had been suspended by the banks.

The innkeeper was not impressed. He pulled out his pistol and took $30 of the paper money from Edward. Then he sent for the local constable while he held his gun on the pair of travelers. The constable came and agreed to ride into the city with them to make certain the paper money was real.

"But the nearest city is Cincinnati," argued Edward. "That's nineteen miles from here."

It was no use. The innkeeper mounted his old mare and the constable joined them for the long ride. Nine miles outside Cincinnati, the innkeeper seemed to be having second thoughts. He stopped in front of Fenton's Tavern and suggested that he would like some breakfast. By this time, Edward and his friend were so angry they refused to stop. Besides, Cincinnati was where they had planned to go that day anyway. The trip was not out of the way for them.

"We insisted on his keeping on to town—which he did. Fasting," said Edward.

They arrived at the city bank at one thirty in the afternoon and had their paper money examined. It was perfectly good, the banker said. The innkeeper returned the thirty paper dollars and Edward had it turned into "hard money." He paid the innkeeper, hoping the coins would feel very heavy all the way back.

"We then left our little wooden squire," he said, "to pay his own expenses and ride home a disagreeable road. And the way he must go, his whole journey would be at least forty-four miles which would cost him—with paying his constable—about $9 or $10 at least. And no satisfaction from us —except our good company."

Exploring

Travelers gave many reasons for taking trips. Some were looking for new land to which they might return with their families and settle down. David Letts had that in mind when he rode his best sorrel mare as far west as Fort Dearborn, looking for just the right spot to settle. One soldier at the fort admired the mare so much that he offered David a large

52

This part of the Natchez Trace was the main road home for travelers who went down the Mississippi River

piece of land in exchange for it. But Letts would not part with his mare. A few years later, David did return west with his family. But the piece of land that he had refused in 1829 is today in the center of Chicago.

Many travelers left home just for the joy of sight-seeing across the huge land that was now their country. Some preferred seeing its cities. Probably the biggest disappointment in the United States was Washington City, the capital.

Washington City had been planned, rather than allowed to grow naturally like European cities and earlier United States cities with crooked streets. In 1805, a traveler said Washington City had wide streets a mile long with no houses on them. Seven years later, another visitor was not impressed with the Capitol building. He reported that it was two large square buildings joined together by a wooden walkway. The walkway was where the large dome and ro-

A modern parkway follows part of the old Natchez Trace

tunda are today. Still later, in the 1840's, Charles Dickens visited Washington. He said, "It has three handsome buildings of marble—all placed as out of the way as possible."

Guidebooks told travelers what to expect when they went sight-seeing. In 1801, Matthew Carey's Pocket Atlas was not limited to just the sights, but included everything from local caves and religions to the species of birds and how many months a person could live in a place without a fire in the fireplace. New England, said the book, had a healthy climate where one person in seven could live to be seventy years old. Philadelphia's streets were straight and crossed each other at right angles, instead of having been laid out along a winding cow path. The atlas also told what sort of people lived in different areas of the United States. New Englanders were "tall, stout, and well built, with handsome women." New Jersey people were "industrious, peaceable, honest and

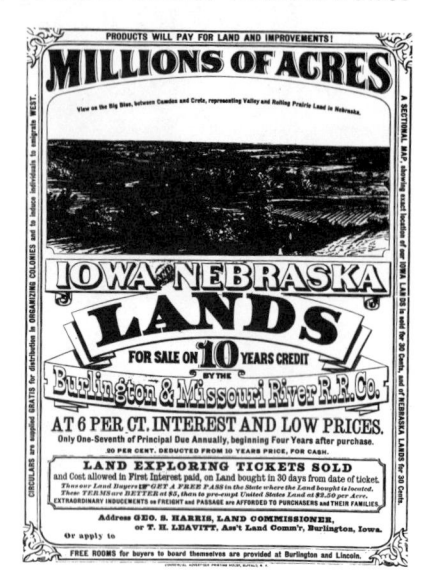

Advertisements like this one
lured travelers farther west

plain in manners." Carolinians were "generally polite, even
tempered and hospitable to strangers"—an early indication
of southern hospitality.

From the first days of travel, Niagara Falls has been the
number one sight-seeing attraction. Descriptions of the Falls
are found in almost every traveler's diary. None of them had
an easy time putting feelings into words as they stood at the
edge of the foaming green and white water.

Annabelle Williams, age eighteen, said, "I came to a complete stand feasting my eyes on the wonderful works of
nature . . . feeling entirely my own insignificance. I can say
with safety that it is indescribable."

"The whirlwind that always rages at the bottom of the
cataract deprived me of breath," said a boy of nineteen. Two
hundred years after the first tourists began telling their
neighbors about Niagara Falls, their descriptions still strike
a nerve in modern sightseers.

Moving Farther West

Horseback travelers returned home after a trip of several months with much new knowledge and satisfaction about their young country. They stood on their porches and noticed the smoke from their neighbor's chimney curling up into the sky. How near the neighbors were getting! Suddenly they began to feel hemmed in by the crowds just as they or their parents had felt when they lived in the east. They could not forget the empty lands they had just seen. Very often, the next trip came soon after the journey on the old horse. But this time, with the whole family going along, travel would have to be on wheels.

3

By Stagecoach and Carriage

Staging It

Roads that were wide enough for four wheels opened up much more of the west for travelers. Luckily, they did not insist on comfort with their travel, knowing that they could not expect that. The only thing these travelers could count on was that nothing would go the way they had planned.

Grant Thorburn had never been out of New York City. So when he read that the New York Jockey Club planned a trip by stagecoach to Albany in the winter of 1831, he decided to go. The advertisement said the trip would be just for club members and was "safe, cheap and comfortable." Thorburn bought a ticket.

Climbing aboard the stagecoach in Hoboken, across the river from New York, Thorburn settled back into the cushions. He would have preferred not to have fifteen other passengers in the coach with him, but he knew that travelers had to expect small discomforts. The passengers thought that this same stagecoach would take them all the way to Albany.

After a few miles, the stagecoach stopped. The driver flung open the door and tossed a mailbag onto the floor. Mailbags were too precious to ride outside in the wintry wind, but any passengers who cared to trade their inside seats for one beside the driver were told they could move. A few miles later, there was another stop. Another mailbag landed on the passengers' knees. Mailbags were added every few miles until the stagecoach reached Hackensack, about eleven miles from the starting point. There the coach stopped at a tavern-grocery-grogshop.

While the passengers were stretching their legs, the driver told them that this particular coach would not be going to Albany, that they should ask the tavernkeeper how they could get to Goshen, New Jersey, where they could find another stagecoach. An hour later, the angry tavernkeeper made arrangements for the marooned travelers. He packed two of them off in an open chair, four in an open wagon, and the rest in a Jersey farm wagon which had loose boards for seats. It began to sleet.

"By the time we got to the next stop," Thorburn said, "we looked like moving pillars of salt. Our hats and coats were covered an eighth inch thick with ice."

The miserable passengers had a chance to thaw out their garments while they had dinner in a tavern on the way to Goshen. But now the sleet turned to snow. They filed out of the warm room unhappily and climbed into something called a "booby hut," the local name for a sort of box on runners. This sleigh, said Thorburn, was no more than a box of wooden boards with spaces between for the wind and snow to blow in. No leather, canvas, or even paint covered the boards. The passengers traveled through the night wondering whether the snow or the rain was worse.

The stage to Klamath Falls, Oregon, stops for an
early morning photograph

"Our cloaks were frozen to one another," said Thorburn.
"In the morning, we looked like some mountain of ice moving down to the Gulf Stream." Thorburn's stagecoach trip
was off to the usual unpredictable start.

Stagecoaches were the cheapest way to travel long distances. The fare was sometimes as little as $3 for a hundred
miles. In addition, a passenger usually paid $1 to sleep at a
stage tavern, which was more expensive than other taverns,
and another 25 cents for dinner.

Stagecoach trips started as early in the day as the driver
wanted to leave—usually at three or four in the morning.
The driver gave his passengers half an hour to stumble from
their beds into the coach, where the horses, already har-

nessed to it, were snorting and stomping with impatience to get away. The first three or four stops were only to change horses. Four or five hours after starting, the stage reached a tavern and the tourists had their first cup of coffee and food.

Horse-changing stops were usually smooth and fast. One passenger said the change was so fast "the coach had not stopped rocking" before they were off again. In the west, however, a wild horse was often broken in by putting it with experienced stagecoach horses. For the travelers, the effect was like having three good wheels and a fourth that wanted to go off in another direction. Eventually, the new horse matched step with the others and the ride was smooth again.

The overland mail coach always drew a crowd of admirers

No stagecoach was ever built for the comfort of the passengers. Surprisingly, the passengers did not demand comfort. Instead, they were serene about traveling.

"Everyone misses something when he travels . . . it is of little consequence whether he was comfortable," said a popular travel book. "However," said Washington Irving when he traveled, "there is some relief in change, even though it be from bad to worse. I have found in traveling in a stagecoach that it is often a comfort to shift one's position and be bruised in a new place."

Something Better

The new Concord coach, built in Concord, New Hampshire, in 1827, made travel more comfortable than anyone had dared to hope. By means of its low center of gravity the Concord coach could round sharp curves at a high speed without turning over too easily. Springy leather straps, called thoroughbraces, helped to relieve the passengers of some of the road shocks. The Concord was built especially for rough American roads which had been known to shake apart European-built coaches. It held fifteen people—nine inside and six outside. In a pinch, it could hold as many as thirty-five. But even though travelers were delighted with the new coach, no one ever said it was comfortable.

Concord coaches were used by the U.S. Mail as well as to carry passengers. The mail coaches could often be seen along the National Road. They had gold-painted sides, each side with a picture of a postboy sitting on a flying horse and blowing his horn. Inside, nine passengers sat on silk plush cushions. Riding in the mail coach was a special treat, even though the coach sometimes detoured into towns to deliver and pick up mail.

Each mail coach passenger bought a ticket for one hundred pounds of weight. A passenger who weighed two hundred pounds or more had to buy two tickets. Each person was allowed only 15 pounds of baggage because the mailbags took up so much space. Mail coach drivers had orders to treat their passengers with the utmost politeness. But they did not have to be at all polite to the driver of a wagon or a cart who was foolish enough to block the way on the road. Nothing must get in the way of the mail stage. The mail driver had the right to see that a slow driver in front of him was arrested in the next town.

Other Wheels

Not all travelers rode in stagecoaches or the mail coach. A traveler who had money and did not like to share the ride could hire "an extra" and drive his family wherever he wanted. Others, like Margaret Dwight, had to ride in a wagon. Margaret was seventeen and was going west to live with relatives she had never seen. They were residing in New Connecticut—today we call it Ohio. Even though she was in no hurry to get there, the trip seemed endless.

"I will never go to New Connecticut with a Deacon again!" said Margaret. "We shall never get there or anywhere else at the rate we go on. We went but 11 miles yesterday and 15 today . . . I'll never go with a Deacon again. We go so slow and so cheap that I am almost tired to death. The horses walk, walk, hour after hour, while the Deacon sits reckoning his expenses and forgetting to drive till some of us ask *when* shall we get there? . . . The reason so few people return from the Western country is not that the country is so good, but because the journey is so bad."

Others, who had started their trip on horseback or just walking, had to settle for whatever vehicle came along the road with four wheels under it. For Francis and Dan Parkman it was a "little carryall," made to seat four people.

Four women, plus baggage, were already in it when the two boys climbed up beside the driver. Since there was no back to their seat, they had to sit bolt upright, because two of the ladies sat back to back with them. The ride was twenty miles—four hours long.

"An attempt on our part to lean back would have pitched the ladies head first into the laps of their neighbors opposite," Francis explained.

As luck would have it, a hard rain began to fall. Francis put up his umbrella to cover Dan and himself. Then they realized that the water they were keeping off themselves was rolling off the umbrella onto the ladies' heads. There was only one thing for gentlemen to do. They put down the umbrella and let the ladies use theirs instead, since there was not space to put up two umbrellas. The water dripped relentlessly down their collars from the ladies' umbrella. But, like all passengers in 1841, they could always hope that the next coach would be more comfortable or that the next piece of road might be better.

Roads and Ruts

Almost all roads were terrible. Even in the middle of good roads, ditches had been dug across for drainage. The ditches caused a coach to bounce and the passengers to jerk forward with a bowing motion. These bumps were called "fall backs" in England and "Thank you, ma'ams" in the United States.

Early dirt roads were very high in the center so that rainwater could drain off. Stagecoaches, already top-heavy with riders, baggage, and sometimes even furniture, tipped dangerously on the curves. A traveler to Baltimore described what it was like:

"For miles the driver was obliged to call to us withinside to balance the car and prevent it from oversetting by stretching our necks out the window on whichever side it rose uppermost . . . Now, gentlemen, to the right . . . Now to the left . . . was continually bawled in our ears."

Some roads had been cut from the forest so fast that stumps were still in the roadbed—some of them sprouting new leaves. When a large rock forced a wheel up, the coach came down with a crash, adding to the bruises on the passengers' backsides. In 1810, one official state highway in Penn-

The horses seem to be disagreeing—which way does the road go?

Mud was a constant problem—in the country

sylvania was actually a creek bed. A stagecoach line that ran along the National Road was known as "the Shake Gut Line" because coaches coming down the road could be heard miles away.

Accidents happened often. Travel guides warned passengers that if they sensed an accident coming, they should hang on to something inside the coach rather than try to jump. Nervous people preferred to ride with the driver so they could jump to safety. One road in the California mountains was so dangerous that stagecoach trips were scheduled there only at night so the passengers could not see the steep drop beside the narrow rocky road.

Mud was the biggest problem. Mudholes appeared in the road whenever it rained. Some were so deep that coach wheels sank up to the boxes. Charles Dickens was horrified at American roads in 1842.

"The road is a series of alternate swamps and gravel pits," he told everyone. "The coach sank down in the mire nearly to the windows, tilted to one side at an angle of 45°, and stuck."

At that, Dickens was lucky. As a first-class passenger, he had the privilege of staying inside while a farmer helped to pull the coach out. Many passengers had to wade into the muck to pull the coaches and horses out of mudholes.

Where a road crossed a swamp, road builders just laid down logs side by side and allowed them to settle. Stage-coach drivers raced over these "corduroy" roads as fast as possible, knowing the logs might sink in deeper if the driver slowed down. Inside, the passengers hung on for dear life.

"The vehicle rose and fell with a violence of motion threatening every moment to hurl me from my seat," said a passenger. Another claimed, "The very slightest of jolts was enough to dislocate all the bones in the human body."

—or in the towns

Crossing Water

Passengers had even more reason to grow tense as the road reached a body of water. Bridges—where there were any bridges—were simply arrangements of wooden planks without nails, laid across two parallel poles. The planks tilted up as the wheels rolled over them.

"American drivers have a complete disregard for human life," groaned one English traveler. "There was a hole in the bridge ahead. I suggested walking the horses across, but the driver used his whip and we dashed ahead."

Later, leaving Philadelphia, this same traveler turned pale when the driver drove onto a "floating bridge" made

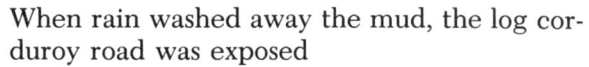

When rain washed away the mud, the log corduroy road was exposed

of large trees chained together. The weight of the carriage made the logs sink and the water came up almost to the door.

Ferryboats were no safer. Often the ferry was only a log raft that had a rickety fence on two sides. One day in 1859, Robert Anderson and his family were crossing the Saluda River in Abbeville, South Carolina. Suddenly, in the middle of the stream, the horse panicked and jumped overboard, taking the carriage with it. The passengers fell into the water and the boatman lost his pole. The ferry, caught in the swollen river, headed toward a dam.

Anderson grabbed his children and swam to safety. A man

Miss Anderson's life was saved by her petticoat in 1859

on shore leaped into a boat and saved Mrs. Anderson. But Anderson's young sister disappeared down the river. Everyone had given her up for lost, when someone shouted from the opposite shore. She was floating high and dry on top of the water. Air had filled her hoopskirted crinoline and kept her floating safely until she was saved. The story was told long afterward, especially by women who defended the wearing of crinolines.

Taverns and Manners

Every forty or fifty miles along a stage route, the coach came to a tavern where the hungry passengers could eat. Each tavern looked much like every other—a long porch, and the tavern walls posted with numerous handbills. In the south, passengers could expect to get "corn bread and common doings" (meaning pork and bacon). In other regions, the "fixings" included great varieties of food. The meal was put on tin plates. The tablecloth of brown canvas seldom met with soap and water.

"We stopped to eat in the middle of the day," said a traveler on the way to Wheeling (then in the state of Virginia). "Passengers ... drivers ... conductors ... sitting down together. We had ham, eggs, enormous crocks of molasses that attracted lots of flies, and negresses waving peacock's tails over the table."

The black slave girls waving the peacock tails did not surprise the travelers nearly so much as having the driver and conductor (who also worked for the stage line) sit down at the same table to eat with them. First-time travelers had much to learn about stagecoach drivers.

The driver was a very important personage at the tavern as well as on the road. He was a golden hero to little boys who watched him as he raced past, sounding his trumpet outside a village. Some drivers were very colorful, like the one Charles Dickens had. That driver dressed like a Russian peasant, said Dickens, in a loose purple robe with fur collar, a multicolored sash around his waist, gray trousers, light-blue gloves, and a bearskin cap.

Tavernkeepers did not serve food on demand. When a

Eating a meal "in public" was a new and strange experience

stagecoach arrived just after a meal had been served, its passengers had to wait until the next time "the cloth was spread" before they could eat. There was plenty of food—meat, chicken, fish, sausages, eggs, and dried beans, all at the same meal. The meal was served when the stage driver sat down. When he finished and wanted to move on, the passengers were finished whether they wanted more to eat or not. Dinner was served in the middle of the day. It was just a short stop between stage rides. Supper, however, was usually at the end of the stage-riding day and the traveler ate where he was going to sleep.

Eating at a tavern was called "having a public dinner." Eating with strangers was very hard for some travelers who could not stand it when table manners of others did not come up to their own standards. One day in 1833, Samuel Breck left the table and wrote this in his diary:

"The foul feeders drove me from the table. I could not keep my seat when a western man fed himself from the celery dish with his knife. The dish was half full of dressed celery. The dirty man took his broad knife from his tobacco mouth, dipped up as much as it would hold, fed himself a half dozen times, and repeated the disgusting custom. On turning my head, my eye caught another chipping the butter with a knife greased by the filth of his mouth. They were all well-dressed and passed for American gentlemen—except at the table."

To Bed—with Company

Stage drivers carried their own bedding. They usually spread it out on the floor after the other travelers had gone upstairs to their beds. The choice place for the driver to sleep was under the table, because then he would not get stepped on during the night. For his night's sleep and the stabling of the horses, the driver paid 75 cents.

Travelers paid one dollar for a bed upstairs. Often there were only two rooms—one for men and one for women. A large tavern had more rooms, but sometimes five or six beds in each one. Strangers shared rooms and sometimes even had to share beds when the tavern was crowded. Foreign visitors were shocked at this togetherness, but innkeepers told them that "it's a custom of the country to which travelers must submit."

The sheets were coarse brown linen and few innkeepers thought it necessary to put more than one sheet on a bed. Sheets were changed only when they were so dirty that a traveler complained loudly. Dirty sheets and bedbugs were all a part of traveling. One traveler was angry at first when an innkeeper told him there was no more room but he could sleep out in the hay beside his horse if he wanted to. Travelers called it "taking the soft side of a barn." The next morning he wrote happily, "Wonderful sleep. There were no bedbugs in the hay!" Probably the barn was also quieter than the inn.

"I must get the habit of sleeping through all manner of noise," said Samuel Breck as he traveled in 1834. "All night, the laughing, talking, singing of servants, slamming of doors, running up and down stairs, arrival and departure of stages, goes on."

Travelers always kept a list of the taverns where they had stopped so they could tell their friends where to stay on a trip. Once in a while, a traveler found a room to himself with a clean bed. More often, tired stage passengers arrived late at night at a tavern filled with emigrants on the way west with their families or with drunks who, after celebrating some sort of holiday, had collapsed in the yard and on the

On the plains where there were no taverns, travelers by overland mail cooked their own meals

stairs. Some innkeepers who did not want to be bothered with "movers" in their taverns put up log huts on the other side of the road. They furnished each hut with a long table, a fireplace, and a couple of benches. The movers did their own cooking, slept on the floor, and paid only 25 cents.

In cities, a hotel was more luxurious. A Cincinnati hotel boasted a piano—the only one in town—to entertain visitors. Barnum's Hotel in Baltimore had curtains around each bed just like hotels in the old country. But the best hotel in the United States was the Tremont House in Boston. It had 200 bedrooms, and there a man could have a room of his own. Tyrone Power tells what a day at the Tremont was like.

"At 7:30 in the morning, the crash of a gong rattles through the remotest galleries to rouse the sleepers," he said.

The breakfast gong rang at eight, although a guest who traveled with a servant was allowed to send his servant down to carry breakfast back up to the room. At three in the afternoon, dinner was served at two long parallel tables, but the meals were only enough "for a man not in a devouring rage," said Power. Tea was served at six in the public rooms, and supper three hours later.

"At first," Power said, "I was worried about eating with 150 people, but I liked it. By 11:00 P.M., the hive is hushed." Unlike a stage tavern, the Tremont remained quiet all night.

Tales About Stage Drivers

Every passenger came home from a trip with a favorite stage driver story. Tyrone Power went from Baltimore to Washington riding on top of a coach. The driver was Mr.

Tolly, and Power could not help admiring his skill. Some of the holes they had bypassed would have swallowed coach and all, Power thought. The wheels were frequently buried up to the hub, and more than once three of the horses were down all of a heap. But with whip and voice, Mr. Tolly had managed to pick them out and put them on their legs again.

"This is a real varmint team you've got hold on, Mr. Tolly," said Power.

"How did you find that out, sir?" exclaimed Tolly.

"Why, it's not hard to tell so much after taking a good look at them, I guess," replied Power.

"Well, that's something! But I guess you're not so far out for once," Tolly answered with a knowing grin of satisfaction. "They are all from Varmont and I am Varmont-born myself as holds 'em. All mountain boys, horses and driver!"

One little boy named Richard had a favorite driver who used to take him to and from boarding school every week. Richard had always wanted to run away to sea—a favorite dream of boys who hated school. On these trips back and forth, Richard always imagined that the stagecoach was the cabin of a ship and the driver was the captain. He thought of the top of the coach as the deck. The fields beside the road were the sea.

One day, as he sat with the captain on the deck, they came to anchor at a tavern. The day was so cold that the driver bought Richard a glass of hot toddy to warm him. But after they were under way again, the driver began to worry that the toddy might have been too strong for the boy. He noticed Richard nodding sleepily and began to fear that the boy might fall asleep and tumble off the high seat next to him. He suggested that Richard go inside the stagecoach, where he would be safe.

"Don't worry," said the boy. "Even if I do fall off, I can swim."

Knowing nothing about Richard's game of sailing, the driver quickly stopped and put the boy inside.

The Ugly Side

There were many stories of robberies, especially in the west. As a rule, stagecoaches in the United States were not robbed nearly so often as those in Europe. That is because most Americans, even in the early days, did not travel with money in their pockets. Instead, they carried bank drafts, bills of exchange, and letters of credit.

One notorious robbery took place on the sand hills of western Nebraska in 1856. One passenger was wounded, but the others escaped safely. Evidently many people wanted to have the notoriety that goes with such an event. When Mark Twain visited the Pacific Coast a few years later, he said he personally met 133 or 134 men who had been wounded during that particular holdup and escape.

"There was no doubt of the truth of it," said Twain. "I had it from their own lips."

Most of the people "staging it" were not on vacations. They traveled for business or to find a new place to move to with their families. Even in the earliest days of the country, some of the travelers worried about the problems of ecology which they could see ahead.

"Passed through a new country," said Charles Leland on his way to Cleveland in 1854. "It was just in the course of clearing . . . there were log houses, log cabins, split logs, burnt logs, hewed logs, hacked logs, and destroyed logs."

Others saw the graffiti in the city. Public seats in the park were covered with sheet iron to preserve them from the "whittling talent common in the U.S." Samuel Breck was upset by the Americans' "inveterate habit of scratching names and figures upon the best buildings and their furniture."

When they traveled, Americans came upon customs in their own country that were as strange to them as if they were in a foreign country. One of these, according to a Pennsylvania senator in 1834, was the custom of parading a famous person (Henry Clay, in this case) through the streets of a city—"a strange way of honoring a man." And the same senator was really upset about another new custom.

"It is much the custom in Harrisburg to introduce strangers to each other and then follows a shake of the hand. I reluctantly submit to this custom of pawing because all the traders, farmers, and even most of the lawyers use their right hands, without handkerchiefs, to blow their noses."

The worst habit of all, according to travelers, was the way the Americans spit. A stage driver claimed he could hit a target as he drove by at top speed. Even well-dressed gentlemen in the cabin of a ship spat on the floor. In the Senate and the House of Representatives in Washington, every honorable member had his spittoon in 1842.

Heading Farther West

The most thrilling moment on a stagecoach ride came when the coach suddenly reached an "artificial road"—one that had been paved by macadamizing. A macadamized road was one made with broken stone and rolled until it was smooth. Now the coach traveled at eight or even ten miles an hour. Hills and trees flew by, and the sounds of the wheels running over the stones made a rhythmic thud-thud that lulled the passengers. The United States did not have many roads to brag about in the early days, but the National Road, which had opened in 1818, was worth traveling many miles just to see. One stage passenger said, "It is a road made for ever."

Travelers who wanted to go very far west had no special road after they reached the end of the National Road. There were only trails that had been well packed down by wagons and coaches that had gone before. By 1865, a stagecoach left from the Missouri River every day, Monday through Saturday, to go to the Rocky Mountains. The trip cost $250 and lasted six days and six nights.

For the first 200 miles, the passengers looked out over prairie land of waving green grass. Gradually they noticed that the soil had become dry and that the green had turned to a brownish color. Now they were on the plains. Streams on the plains were few and far between, but the drivers knew where to find safe drinking water. Traffic was thick with wagon trains going in the same direction and an occasional wagon going back toward the east. Wagons lumbered along at four miles an hour, while the stagecoaches went twice as fast, stopping to change horses every ten or twelve miles. The passengers had nothing to do but get acquainted.

"What was something," said one tourist, "there was not two persons from the same state among our eight passengers. A more jolly crew, I guess, never happened together. First there was a small sample of Kentucky, a short chap about 6 foot 6 inches. He was very good looking, manly, full of fun and jolly as he could be. Next was a South Carolina

Episcopal minister who was a short, thick sort of chap. The first day or two, he put on an austere sedate countenance. He would not enjoy himself in our company in hopes we would look up to him as something more than common. But he found himself mistaken. We kept on with our jokes.

"Next was a Virginian, a doctor by profession, who was as kindly as a kitten. Next was a native of Alabama. He was sociable and an excellent traveling companion. Next was from Tennessee and he could carry on his end of the jokes very well. The Bostonian in the group was an artful, cunning knave. The Pennsylvanian was a Quaker's son—the wildest little devil I most ever saw. As for the Jersey man, a description of him will be needless. According to the old rule 'if you cannot say anything good of him, say nothing.'"

A trip seemed much shorter in a jolly crowd. Travelers had a new audience for their stories and jokes every time they changed coaches. One old favorite, sure to get a chuckle at least, was about the sign a farmer had put beside the road. The sign read:

"I will give one acre of land FREE to any man who is really content."

One man decided to take the farmer up on his offer and so called at his house.

"I've come for the acre of land," he announced.

"Are you truly content with your life?" asked the farmer.

"That I am," the man answered.

"Then, if you're so content, what do you want with my land?" said the farmer and shut the door.

Every forty or fifty miles, the westbound Concord coach stopped at a "rancho" so the passengers could eat. Ranchos were no improvement over taverns in the east. They were usually built of adobe, with dirt floors. Often the only light was from candles. At a rancho, travelers could buy such supplies as liquor, fruit, knives, playing cards, saddles, and even blue-green goggles to wear on sunny days. When there were not enough chairs, the guests sat on their own luggage. They carried their own eating utensils, too, because there were rarely enough spoons to go around.

"As the customers left," one woman said, "their dishes were wiped out for us to use. There was too much saleratus in the biscuits—they were bitter and green in color."

Meals at the rancho usually included bacon, eggs, biscuits, green tea, coffee, dried peaches, dried apples, beef, antelope, and whatever vegetables were around. A standard comment at the table was, "If you don't like the food, help yourself to the mustard."

The All-Night Coach

Ranchos had no space for overnight guests, and for five hundred miles there were no taverns where travelers could spend a night. So the stagecoaches traveled all night. The tourists ached for a place to stretch out their legs and have one good night's sleep. This is what one man had to say about his trip west:

"Dreary weariness comes over the coach-crowding passengers. The air gets cold. The road grows dusty and chokes you. The legs become stiff and numb. The temper edges. Everybody is overcome with sleep but can't stay asleep. Everybody flounders and knocks about against everybody else in helpless despair. Perhaps the biggest man in the stage will really get asleep—which doing he involuntarily and with irresistible momentum, spreads himself, legs, boots, arms and head, over the whole inside of the coach. The girls screech. The profane swear. Some lady wants a smelling-bottle out of her bag and her bag is somewhere on the floor. Nobody knows where, but found it must be. Everybody's back hair comes down, and what is nature and what is art in costume and character is revealed. And then, hardest trial of all, morning breaks upon the scene and the feelings. Everybody dirty, grimy, faint, 'all to pieces,' cross—such a disenchanting exhibition!"

When the stagecoach stopped at a western town that had a hotel, life did not improve much. The hotels were not at all like the inns and hotels back east. The walls were of thin canvas, sometimes decorated with wallpaper pasted onto the canvas. The light did not shine through much, but the sounds from the next room were very clear. Men slept on one side of a large room. Women slept on the other. Mattresses and pillows were flour sacks stuffed with straw. In the one public washroom was a dirty tin washbasin, a lump of homemade soap in an empty can, and one wet dirty towel on a roller for everyone to use.

Mania for Speed

When improvements finally came for people traveling in stagecoaches, the progress was not in the direction of comfort. Foreign travelers had always noticed the "American mania for speed." No matter how fast travel was, someone always wanted to get there faster. Speedier stagecoaches were the answer—but horses could travel only at a limited speed.

"The Flying Machine" cut the travel time between Phila-

In 1905, Yellowstone Park travelers were still using stagecoaches and tallyhos

delphia and New York City by several hours—by not leaving from New York at all. Advertisements posted in both cities announced that the new service would take "a day and a half." The cost was $6.50, including meals, for the "inside" passenger, a little less if one sat outside. The passenger from New York took a little boat that landed him in Amboy, New Jersey, several hours later at 3 A.M. Then he boarded the stagecoach and began counting his "day and a half."

"The Flying Diligence" soon outdistanced "The Flying Machine" by not stopping to allow its passengers to eat. Now the trip could be made in only sixteen hours. Today the trip takes about two hours by an automobile obeying the speed limit.

Stagecoach drivers could not believe they would be replaced by that "teapot on a track," as they called the railroads. Steam boilers and engines often exploded and many travelers were not willing to risk their necks at first. But eventually it was obvious that if a traveler wanted to move fast, the stagecoaches were never going to progress. The railroads might.

Stagecoaches did not die fast. Long after automobiles were on the roads, travelers were still saying, "The stagecoach will never be replaced—especially in the mountains." Neither railroads nor automobiles could go up mountains at first. In the 1920's, visitors to Yellowstone Park were still traveling by stagecoach to see the sights.

4

ALONG THE DITCHES BY CANALBOAT

Canal Fever

"I never saw people packed so close as they were that night in the canalboat's saloon," said Jonathan Fish. "Mattresses completely covered the floor, on which people lay as close as possible. The dinner table was covered with sleeping humanity more thickly than Captain Davis ever strewed it with beefsteaks. And those who lay under the table thought themselves favored, inasmuch as they could not be trodden upon."

Fish had slipped the captain an extra dollar so he could have a berth near the door. The other passengers pulled numbers out of a hat for their berths. As usually happened, the fattest passengers drew the highest bunks and were urgently pressed by those who were to sleep underneath them to trade places.

During the day, the canalboat ride had been peaceful, but the summer sun had beaten down unmercifully to heat the tiny cabin like an oven. The boat rode so low in the water that no breeze came, even after dark, to cool

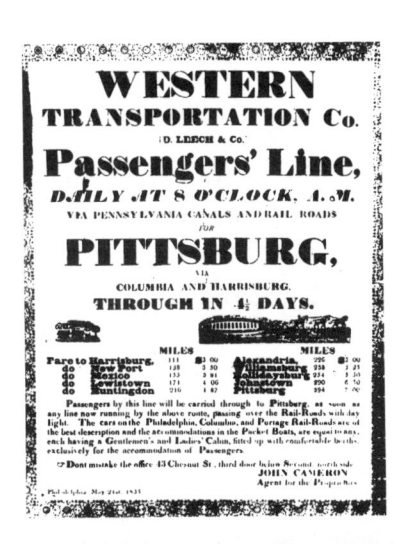

Erie Canalboat riders paid $7 for the fastest route to Pittsburgh from Philadelphia as promised in this 1835 advertisement

it. The air in the cabin was stifling.

Canals had been very successful in Europe. Some of the earliest immigrants to arrive in America had said that building canals would end this country's travel problems. The first small canals appeared in the early 1800's. Interest grew fast. By 1825, when the Erie Canal was completed, most Americans had "canal fever" and could hardly wait to try the newest way to travel farther west. William Davidson took his family on their first canalboat ride in Pennsylvania that year.

"Our boat was built this year," he said. "A rough affair—much inferior to the boat in which we traveled on the New York canal two years ago. [Only a portion of the Erie Canal had been finished then.] Breakfast was prepared in a very rough style. One of the passengers, a sea captain, took charge of superintending it as the regular cook was absent. It was served up in unusual style, the kettle placed on a table uncovered by a cloth and everybody taking care of himself."

By the 1850's, a traveler could go from New York City to a city on the Ohio River (over a thousand miles) almost entirely by water. He took a boat up the Hudson River to Albany and boarded an Erie Canal boat to Buffalo. There he boarded a boat crossing Lake Erie to Cleveland and changed to a canalboat to Portsmouth on the Ohio River. The trip knocked days off the overland journey where wagons had to cross the Allegheny Mountains. Freight sent by the canal and lake route took 20 days instead of 30 days and cost only half as much as sending it with wagoners. One reason the canal and lake route was faster was that the boats kept moving all night as well as all day.

Other travelers, finding a better way west, stayed on the Lake Erie boat until it reached Toledo. There they boarded the country's most luxurious canalboat down the Wabash and Erie Canal. The packet *Silver Bell* was painted silver, decorated with silver bells, and pulled by silver-gray mules. It traveled eight to ten miles an hour. When the passengers landed in Terre Haute, Indiana, they hired a coach or bought a wagon to carry them as far west as Missouri along the National Road. They were well on their way to the start of the California-Oregon Trail with little mud on their boots, no mountains to cross, and in half the normal time.

Mule or Horse Power

Canal travel was not for people in a hurry. The boats were usually pulled by mules at the rate of two or three miles an hour. Most canals had a speed limit of not more than four miles an hour, because backwash from fast-moving boats ruined the canal's sides.

"But there is no chance of getting one's neck broke as there is aboard those stages," added an admirer of the new system. "And if the boat sinks, one's only up to one's knees in water."

The traveler who wanted to move his whole family cheaply chose an emigrant, or line, canalboat. The family took along a stove and cooked their own meals. They slept on the floor, but then so did some of the travelers on the expensive packet boat. If they did not cook their own food, the line boat travelers shared the simple diet of the boat's crew—bread, fried bacon, and black coffee.

Occasionally this diet was enriched by the alert eye of the "hoggie." The hoggie was the young boy hired ($30 for half a year) to walk along by the plodding mules and keep them moving. President James A. Garfield was a hoggie along the Ohio Canal as a teen-ager. One of the hoggie's extra duties was to keep his eyes open for fresh ears of corn, ripe fruits, or a stray chicken. Farmers who lived along the canal claimed that they planted the first three rows "for the canalers," knowing very well they would help themselves to the food anyway. But a farmer relentlessly chased any hoggie who stole a board from his fence to use in the boat's stove.

The most comfortable way to travel along the canals was by packet boat. Packets had names like *Water Witch* and *Gliding Susan* until speed became very important. Then the packets used horses instead of mules. Fresh horses were stabled at regular relay points along the canal. By changing horses every ten or twelve miles, a packet could make well over 80 miles a day. The 4-mile-an-hour speed limit was

A canal packet boat could make 80 miles a day unless the traffic was snarled

completely ignored and the cost of the fine was added to the passenger's fare. With speed came new boat names like those of Atlantic clipper ships—*Greyhound* and *Flying Cloud.*

The packet traveler paid twice as much as the line, or emigrant, boat passenger. After 1825, packet travel cost 4 cents a mile, including breakfast. If the passenger preferred, he could pay 3 cents a mile and then pay 37½ cents for dinner, 25 cents for breakfast, and 12½ cents for lodging. Breakfast on a good packet included fried ham, liver, sausage, salmon, beets, pickles, pudding, dark bread and butter, maple sugar, and tea. For dinner, the passengers could choose from four or five kinds of fowl and meat, half a dozen kinds of hot breads, vegetables, and seven or eight kinds of pie and cake.

Packet passengers were allowed to carry only the bags they could hold in their hands. The space that was saved by not having heavy baggage was filled with bodies. No packet captain felt guilty about filling the space intended for thirty passengers with a hundred people of all sizes. Instead, he bragged of the feat.

One day a stagecoach carrying Harriet Beecher Stowe arrived at a canalboat landing.

"There's the boat!" one passenger exclaimed. A dozen travelers stuck their heads out of the stagecoach windows and uttered cries of horror at the tiny size of the boat.

"We can't half of us get into that!"

"*We,* indeed," said an experienced traveler who had been on a canalboat before. "I think you'll find it will hold us and a dozen more loads like us."

When the new passengers went below, they discovered that already there was a large group of old ladies, babies, mothers, big baskets, and carpetbags in the ladies' cabin.

"Then," said Mrs. Stowe, "after us follows an indiscriminate raining down of all shapes, sizes, sexes, and ages, men, women, children, babies, nurses . . . 'We shall be smothered' . . . 'We shall be crowded to death' . . . 'We can't stay here' . . . are heard faintly from one and another. And yet, though the boat grows no wider, the walls no higher, they do live and do bear it, in spite of repeated protestations to the contrary."

Hotel Afloat

Most packets had narrow saloons, about ten feet long, that were high enough to allow a man under six feet tall to stand up. The nicest boats had heavy velvet curtains separating the ladies' sleeping area from the end used by the gentlemen. But where there was no such refinement, the gentlemen stood on the deck at bedtime (even when it was raining) until the ladies had undressed and were bedded down. Then the men came down and curled up in the remaining spaces.

During the day, the long table in the center was used for meals. At night it was piled with clothing, bonnets, boots, umbrellas, portmanteaus, baskets, and anything else the owners were sure to want to find in the middle of the night. The side benches became beds at night—for the lucky passengers. Those who drew unlucky numbers slept in two or three tiers of canvas or metal shelves about twelve inches wide. These were suspended from the ceiling by cords or thin chains. In 1842, Charles Dickens described his first night in an American canalboat.

"I was in some uncertainty and doubt at first, relative to the sleeping arrangements on board this boat. I remained in the same vague state of mind until ten o'clock or thereabouts. Then, going below, I found suspended on either side of the cabin, three long tiers of hanging bookshelves, designed apparently for volumes of the small octavo size. Looking with greater attention at these contrivances (wondering to find bookshelves in such a place), I noticed on each shelf a sort of microscopic sheet and blanket. Then I began dimly to comprehend that the passengers were the library

A schoolteacher shows her children life on a canalboat near Washington, D.C., 1899

. . . and that *we* were to be arranged edgewise on these shelves till morning."

Since sleeping was almost impossible anyway, it hardly mattered that the shelves were too narrow for the occupants to turn over. Babies cried. The boat scraped into and out of locks during the night. Noises from the canalside taverns and the horse-exchange stations, added to the swearing and fighting at the locks, kept sleep just out of reach. Then, just as drowsiness came, the captain called below.

"Chambermaid! Wake up that lady who wants to be set ashore!"

The lady and her two children leaped up, stepping on bodies across the floor, fumbling for bonnets, shoes, gloves, shawls, and the little boy's cap, each of which seemed to have fallen in a different spot.

Early in the morning, any person who had managed to fall asleep was wakened by the steward, who must make up the room before breakfast could be served. The passengers stumbled on deck to wash in a bucket of canal water. They used the public comb and brush, and shared the one towel set out for all to use. After breakfast, the steward turned barber and, at one end of the dining table, he shaved the men and cut their hair.

Some passengers hopped off for a brisk walk alongside the towpath. While the boat was going through a lock (about ten minutes), there was time for shopping. The lockkeeper's wife often sold pies, cakes, and fresh vegetables to the travelers. Some packets carried books for the passengers to read. Other passengers entertained themselves with games of their own. At one end of the table were games of whist, backgammon, and draughts. Sometimes there was singing or reading aloud. Often there were debates over politics.

But a favorite entertainment was betting on the races. The racecourse was the long dining table. The racers were bed-bugs, frogs, or grasshoppers—kept under a teacup until the starting gun.

On the upper deck were some low-backed seats called "settles." The overflow sat on the cabin roof—temporarily. The bridges over the canal had been made as low as possible to save money. Anyone sitting up on the cabin roof when passing under a bridge was in danger of getting a crushed skull.

"It was rather amusing to hop down and then to hop up

A canalboat passenger risked losing his head if a low bridge came along when he wasn't looking

again," said an English traveler his first day on the boat. "But by and by, this skipping about became very tiresome and marred the tranquillity of the day very much."

The cry of "Low bridge!" was heard three hundred times in just the first two days of travel along the Erie Canal.

Rules and Rulebreakers

Passenger packets had the right-of-way on the canals. Other boats steered to the far right and lowered their towlines so they would not become entangled with the ropes from the packet. Right-of-way at the locks was often decided by muscle. Captains of rival packet boats hired the toughest crews they could find and let them slug it out at the lock. One stretch of canal between Albany and Schenectady was called "the battleground."

The captain of a packet boat was an important man in his community. He was paid $60 a month. However, the captain of an emigrant boat that carried freight was often short-handed and had to do many of the crew's jobs himself. Both captains had to be good-natured because it was very easy for their crews to "jump ship." Any farmer who wanted to be a captain could build himself a boat and push it out into the canal. Until well into the 1900's, many men earned their living carrying freight and passengers on the canal. Their families lived on the boats with them.

Traffic became very heavy. The summer of 1826, over 19,000 boats and rafts passed the town of West Troy on the Erie Canal. Rules for using the canal had to be written down. First, all boats had to carry lights at night. Each packet had two large whale-oil reflector lanterns. Next, every boat had

Life on a canalboat—Mama can wash the clothes without worrying since her children are chained to the boat

to be registered and had to have the name painted on it in letters four inches high. Boats with sharp, square bows had to have something on the bow to protect other boats they might ram into. Every boat had to have some sort of guard attached to its keel so that the lowered towlines of the boats it was passing could not catch on the rudder. Every boat also had to have a knife on both the bow and the stern to cut apart any towrope that was illegally passed over a deck.

Accidents and Problems

Tangled towlines caused some serious accidents. Once H. J. Heinz was helping a friend move by canalboat when a tangled towline caught the horse he was riding and pulled the horse into the water underneath the boat. Heinz jumped off the horse just in time.

Sometimes the steersman turned the boat too suddenly and pulled a horse into the water. Children fell from boats sometimes or were hurt as the boats went into the locks. Canalers who traveled with little children secured them on the boat with a length of belt or chain.

A break in the canal could cause a traffic jam of boats many miles long, a jam that might take two weeks to clear up. Once when a coal boat stuck sideways in a canal, the captain of a packet boat said that he knew how to shake it loose. He collected all the horses he could find and fastened them to his boat's towlines. Then he backed up and started racing those horses as fast as they could go. They pulled his boat along so rapidly that a great wave of water was built up. When the swell hit the coal boat, the stuck boat was jarred loose. The traffic moved on down the canal.

Occasionally a very serious accident happened—such as the time the bottom fell out of an aqueduct. The aqueduct was a canal-carrying bridge that crossed over a creek. It was filled with water so a canalboat could drift across. When the bottom fell out of an Erie Canal aqueduct, five canalboats fell through the hole to the creek below.

Sometimes it was the mania for speed that made captains careless. Instead of waiting for floodwaters to go down when their canalboats had to cross a fast-moving stream, some captains went ahead. They crossed through and the swift current hit the canalboat broadside. There was nothing to keep the little flatboat from being swept downstream—and in some cases over a dam—except the taut ropes fastened to the horses on a towpath bridge.

Collisions with other boats were common. One night Carl

Arfwedson was trying to sleep on his twelve-inch shelf when he found himself flying through the air.

"A sudden thump against my side of the boat spread consternation among the travelers. The beams cracked. The doors flew open. About a dozen sleeping individuals were thrown from the second and third tiers onto the unfortunate beings who were lying on the floor. One cord gave way after another. The ladies rushed in among us. All were running, shoving against each other, swearing and making a noise in the dark. Confusion, in short, was at its height, until the

The best part of living on a canalboat was diving into the canal right off the back porch

Captain made a favorable report which restored tranquillity."

During the day, the passengers enjoyed watching the other traffic along the canal. Emigrant boats, pulled by old nags, moved twenty to forty miles a day. Families moving west were piled into cheaply built boats with little cabins on top and pulled by the family oxen. Shantyboats were anchored in the canal—they were going nowhere, as they had nothing to pull them. Timber rafts were much in the way of traffic. Trade boats, floating saloons, museum boats, and bookstore boats kept the travelers amused. Barnes's Department store was a boat that moved along the Pennsylvania canals. Performances by minstrels, magicians, trained dogs, monkeys, and white mice arrived in small canalside towns by way of three showboats. When the three boats were fastened together side by side, they opened up to form one large theater.

The Erie Canal

Many states had canals and peaceful rivers that could be used by canalboats. The traveler had many choices of ways to go—all of them slow. The best-known trip, however, was up the Hudson River from New York City and then across the state to Buffalo.

The river traveler carried with him a pocket guidebook that told him in which direction he should be looking at any given moment. Distances, the book explained, had been measured when the waters were frozen and so could not be disputed. Here are just a few of the highlights one could watch for on the trip up the Hudson River:

"at 1 mile, on right, see City Hall

at 2½ miles, on right, pass State Prison

at 5¼ miles, on right, pass Botanic Gardens

at 8 1/3 miles, on right pass Manhattanville, on left Palisadoes, 170 feet high

at 10 miles, on left, Fort Lee and Palisadoes, 311 feet high

Mules pull a canalboat from the lower of five locks in Lockport, N.Y.

at 11 miles, on right, Fort Washington of Revolutionary
War

at 12½ miles, on left, the 'English neighborhood'

at 21½ miles, on left, Palisadoes 550 feet high and the
New York-New Jersey line

at 33 miles, on right, Mt. Pleasant or Sing Sing

at 44 miles, Horse Race (a dangerous place)

at 52½ miles, on left, West Point U.S. Military Academy
and Fort Putnam

at 72½ miles, on left, Halfway Place

at 81½ miles, on right, Hyde Park

at 86 miles, on left, Indian Face

at 112 miles, on left, Catskill Dock. The Kaatsbergs, or
Catskill Mountains, on the left are 8 to 12 and 20 miles
distant from the River along here, elevated 3,000
feet. Regular stages in Summer twice a day, fare $1.

at 145 miles, on left, Albany."

Another book told the traveler just what to look for along
the Erie Canal, where to get out to see such natural wonders
as waterfalls, and what stages he could get from each of the
small towns along the route. Between Albany and Schenectady were 27 locks and 2 aqueducts. But careful reading of
the book showed a traveler how to save 21 hours of travel
time by taking a stagecoach straight to Schenectady and
boarding the canalboat there.

The country west of Schenectady was so wild that before
the canal was built, it took 29 days just to travel 50 miles.
Another sight to watch for was the Montezuma Swamp. The
canal builders had had to wait until winter when the ground
was frozen before they could dig there. Then they invented
a kind of cement that hardened underwater. In the summer,

the horses and mules walked on a wooden bridge almost a mile long, pulling the boat through four-foot-high grass in a marsh filled with ducks, birds, and mosquitoes.

Tyrone Power once asked the captain of his boat if the mosquitoes would be like that all the way to Albany as he traveled east.

"No, siree," was the answer. " 'Twon't be like this all the way to Albany. Oncet we get into the 50-mile Cedar Swamp, 'twill be considerable worser, but not nigh so bad as what 'twill be in the Long Swamp. Them's actual galinippers yonder."

Galinippers in 1801 were mosquitoes that took a gallows-sized nip or a bite big enough to kill.

Towns along the Erie Canal had sprung up so suddenly that they were not ready for city status. Rochester had grown so fast that the merchants were doing business before they had roofs over their heads. The mud in the main street was up to a person's knees after a rain. So many tree stumps and alder bushes grew in the middle of the street in 1830 that a stagecoach took almost an hour to go the two miles through the center of town.

Between Rochester and Lockport was "the Long Level." For sixty-three miles, from sunup to sundown, the passengers did not see a single lock. Then, in Lockport, there were five locks in a row carrying boats uphill and five others carrying boats down. These locks had been carved out of solid rock. Tourists going to Niagara Falls left the boat at Lockport to take a stage to Lewiston.

The canal ended in the town of Tonawanda. From there, it was only a few miles to Buffalo. The passengers had traveled 145 miles up the Hudson River and another 363 miles across New York State by canal. During the trip, they had gone through 83 locks and crossed 18 aqueducts. And at the western end of the canal, they stood only 568 feet higher than they had been on the Hudson River.

Pennsylvania's Canals

Pennsylvanians were not happy when they saw all the traffic, freight as well as people, going to New York State. Philadelphia was suddenly no longer the first seaport in the nation—New York City was. The wagoners who had crossed the mountains for years were most unhappy about rumors that a canal was to be built in Pennsylvania. But it was the only solution.

One began a trip on the westbound section of the Pennsylvania Canal by going to the canal office in Philadelphia the night before. Rising before daybreak, the traveler first experienced a 118-mile boat ride on dry land. The canalboat was divided into two segments. Each segment was mounted on wheels. With the passengers sitting inside, the horses dashed off into the west pulling the canalboat behind. The first night was spent at Lancaster, Pennsylvania. Next morning at two, the passengers were back in their canalboat "train" for the final dash to the town of Columbia on the Susquehanna River. At four o'clock on the third morning the canalboat sections had been put together into one long boat. As soon as the passengers boarded, the boat began moving slowly by being poled up the Susquehanna River to the first lock. Beyond Harrisburg, where the Juniata River joins the Susquehanna River, was a two-story towpath. One level was for eastbound horses and mules. The other level was for those westbound. But there were more surprises to come.

Pennsylvania canalboats came apart in the middle to be loaded onto cars and pulled up a mountain by a steam winch in Portage, Pa.

In the early fall of 1834, Jesse Christman had decided to move with his family to Illinois. However, instead of loading the family and belongings into a wagon, he put them all in a boat, which he named *The Hit or Miss.* He knew the canal ended at Hollidaysburg, where there was a mountain almost 1,400 feet high. He planned to sell his boat when he arrived there and ship his goods and family on the Allegheny Portage Railroad to the town of Johnstown. There he would buy another boat and continue on his way west.

When the Christman family arrived in Hollidaysburg, someone suggested that Mr. Christman just put his boat on a flatbed railroad car and haul it over the mountain to Johnstown. Others had thought of the idea, but no one had ever tried it. When Christman's *Hit or Miss* rode safely up the

inclined railway and down the other side, the idea was
adopted for all canalboats.

After that day, the traveler from Philadelphia to Pittsburgh sat in his piece of canalboat while it was hauled up the
several stages on the inclined railway. When he reached the
top of the mountain, he spent the night at an inn before
continuing downhill. Annabel Williams was a teen-ager
when she and her family traveled over the inclined railway,
known as the Allegheny Portage Railroad.

"We passed over the mountains by means of ten inclined
planes," she explained. "There were five up and five down.
All moved by stationary engines, except one which we came
down by means of Centre of Gravity! It was about five miles
long and we moved very rapidly in the mountains, being at

Canals were peaceful, but travel on them was
not fast enough for Americans

a considerable distance above the clouds which we saw sailing beneath us."

After a night at the inn, westbound passengers continued down the Allegheny Portage Railroad, going through a 900-foot long tunnel under a mountain. When they were once again in a canalboat on the water, they headed downstream on the Conemaugh and Kiskiminetas Rivers, passing through another very long tunnel. It was arched with hewn stone and solid rock. To some of the travelers, even the word "tunnel" was new. All of them felt as awed as Annabel.

"The earth was about 200 feet above our heads and there was a large house and farm on top of it. A well was dripping down on our heads."

Other states had canals, too. Each one was a marvel of engineering. But canals had come too late. The peace and tranquillity that travelers found along the quiet waters were only a source of annoyance for Americans who wanted to get from here to there as fast as possible. Just as the canals were ready to do business, the railroad steam engine arrived. Everyone knew that canalboats could never go fast. The railroad did promise speed. Canals could never take people all the way west. Railroads could. Travelers deserted the packet boats and boarded railroad cars instead.

5

Drifting Downstream by Flatboat

Danger Ahead

John Philips looked out at the murky Mississippi River and wondered how on earth he happened to be sitting on this log at this place on a raw November 22 in 1826. He was young and eager for adventure—but not this kind of adventure.

"Passing Plum Point (a very snaggy place), we had the misfortune to snag one of our boats," he wrote in his diary. "Had to land all the boats on a sand bar to keep the snagged boat from sinking, as well as the other boat that was fastened to it. We were able to stop the leaks in a partial manner in a few minutes after landing. Rigged two pumps and repaired the hole. Then we found we had sunk aground in such a bad place it will be with difficulty we get off."

The next day, all three boats were hard aground. The small crew pushed, pulled, and dug without success. Out on the river, other boats passed by without any offers of help. Three days later, a steamboat went aground just a mile above the helpless flatboats and another hit the bottom just below them. But, even though both steamboat crews promised help when their own ships were free, they went on down the river without so much as a good-by wave to the flatboaters.

The fifth day aground, the inexperienced crew rigged an anchor to help pull the flatboats off. But the small skiff they were using overturned and filled with water, almost drowning the captain, who could not swim. Now the water began going down, leaving the three flatboats higher on the land than ever. Several other boats ran aground. Each time the crew went to help the newly snagged boats, the men returned with a few extra hands to try to help to get their own boats off the bar. But the boats would not move. Finally one

A flatboat family learns *how* by hard experience

old boatman told the rest of the crew they should unload their boats to float them off and then reload them.

"By 9:00 A.M. [on the tenth day after they had grounded], all the boats were handsomely under sail," Philips said. They moved out into the 3½ mile an hour current. "We bid good-bye to Plum Point and Desolation Sand Bar. At 3:00 P.M., struck another snag with the boat and punched another hole in her. But this time were careful to land in a good place."

Philips and his friends were learning about flatboating on the rivers through hard experience. That was the only way to learn about travel downstream. No one had written any books on just how to handle riverboats. The flatboaters had, however, read a book telling them they could travel 2,200 miles down the Ohio and Mississippi Rivers for as little as five or ten dollars for a whole family, not counting the cost of the boat and supplies. But the travel book never actually told its readers *how* the trip was to be made. Yet it started thousands of poor Americans traveling farther west, using the river currents for power.

Most people believed the trip would be cheap, fast, and easy. They planned to load the farm animals on board and so have eggs, milk, and meat with them. Plenty of water was available just by dipping a pan over the side. The trip was sure to be as fast as the river currents moved the boat—and that was even faster after the spring rains made the rivers flood. The travelers would have no bumpy, muddy roads to cope with, no sick horses to slow their trips, no huge waves to make them seasick. Not even Indians or river pirates were serious dangers along the Ohio River after 1800. Once having boarded their boats, the flatboaters imagined they could just sit back and coast downriver all the way to their destinations. They would have one long holiday—with, maybe, some good fishing from the back of the boat.

The flatboat travelers knew less about their trip ahead than any other kind of traveler. Hardly anyone who had ever gone downstream with his family had ever come back up to tell others what to expect. The travelers knew only that they had to reach a starting place along any river that eventually flowed into the Ohio or Mississippi.

Getting to the River

Southerners took a stagecoach from Baltimore to Wheeling on the Ohio River. They paid $17.25 each for the ride across the best piece of highway in the United States—the National Road. They marveled at its stone bridges, iron mileposts, and iron gates where the turnpike fee was collected. Its macadamized surface was so smooth that coaches sometimes moved along as fast as ten miles an hour.

Before reaching Wheeling, the National Road went through the town of Brownsville in Pennsylvania. Brownsville was on the Monongahela River which flowed north to join the Ohio River. There some of the best flatboats were built. Many westbound travelers left the stagecoach at Brownsville. There they bought their boats, stocked up on supplies, and began the river journey toward the west by floating north to Pittsburgh.

Pittsburgh is on a point of land where the Monongahela and the Allegheny River (from the north) join to form the Ohio River which flows west. Pittsburgh, for that reason, was called the "Gateway to the West." Most flatboat adventurers headed for the "Gateway" to start the holiday part of their journeys. From New York State, travelers came down the

Allegheny River by flatboat. But most of the travelers came straight across the state of Pennsylvania from the east.

Several rows of mountains, called the Alleghenies, stretched across the state, cutting off Pittsburgh from cities in the east. The Alleghenies can be crossed today by automobile in a few hours, but in those days, the mountains might as well have been the Alps. They were the highest mountains most Americans had ever seen and were filled with unknown terrors. The valleys all ran in the wrong direction. There was no way to get past them except to climb up one mountain, down the other side, and up the next.

"Pittsburgh is 300 miles from Philadelphia," complained one traveler, "and 150 of them are mountains."

A man could buy a horse for about $80 in the east and travel at his own speed across the mountains in about a week. However, some travel book writers made the Alleghenies sound much more terrifying than they really were. Thomas Ashe, who crossed them with a horse in 1806, said he was trapped at the top of one mountain with night falling and not a place of safety in sight.

"If I attempted to advance," said Ashe, "sudden and rapid death was unavoidable. And if I remained, the wolves, panthers and tiger cats would devour me."

He reminded his readers that just because the traveler did not hear any panthers around or had not seen one was no reason to feel safe.

"The panther is not idle," he told his trusting readers. "He is never heard till in the act of springing on his victim when he utters a horrid cry."

Ashe's book convinced many families that the only safe way to travel to Pittsburgh was by stagecoach over the mountains at a cost of $20 for each person. They shipped their worldly goods by Conestoga freight wagon—to arrive at the head of the Ohio River just in time to start the boat trip. Then they climbed into the stagecoach for the eight-day trip over the mountains. The trip might have been bearable during the summer, but one of the tricks of flatboating was to arrive at Pittsburgh in time to descend the river on the spring flood. So the stagecoach trip was made in snow, ice, and bone-chilling winds.

Buying a Flatboat

The flatboaters' education began when they reached the rivers. Along the ice-encrusted edges they found hundreds of tiny wooden shacks, all filled with people. These were the flatboat families waiting to take off as soon as the ice melted and the floes floated downstream. The traveler lodged his family in a good tavern, which cost 50 cents a day, including three meals, and went to buy a flatboat.

Flatboats came in all styles for all prices. Salesmen pointed out their prize models that "could float on a heavy dew." Some builders tried to convince the buyer that he must buy a tougher boat if he intended to enter the Mississippi River. Still another warned the confused traveler that he would never make it past the dreaded "Falls of the Ohio" if he bought a boat that was too wide. A day later, another boat-builder would tell him he needed a very large boat that would hold three or four families. With more families, the man argued, there would be company for the wives and children on the long trip and more men to share the heavy work of steering, the long night watches, and the hunt for food.

Keelboats were a little more expensive than flatboats, but safer. They were pointed at both ends and built of strong oak. The keelboat bow would not shatter when the boat hit a rock or tree. Keelboats had the added advantage of being able to go upstream in case the traveler changed his mind and wanted to retrace his way. Or at the end of his trip the traveler could sell his keelboat to a buyer who was going upstream. At any rate, everyone who planned to go any distance down the Mississippi River bought a keelboat instead of a flatboat.

Most travelers paid about $130—about three dollars for each foot in length—for a flatboat and just a little more for a keelboat. Both types needed at least three strong men on

Arks were flatboats as big as houses

board—one to steer with the long sweep that acted as a rudder and one man on each side to work the long poles and keep the boat in the deep water. The polemen had to be constantly alert to keep the boat from running aground or from being swept downstream sideways.

Choosing a good boatbuilder was important. Many were dishonest. Sometimes, under the waterline, the seams in boats were stuffed with tow—or any other material that would stick tight between the planks. Above the waterline, there was often no stuffing and water seeped in with every storm-swept wave. Some builders used rotting planks or wood that had knots. The pressure from the water soon pushed out the knots and then the boat had instant round holes. Most boats had no iron in them at all—their planks were held together with wooden pins or treenails made of white oak. When one careless boatbuilder was sued by a furious customer, the judge nodded sympathetically. The judge told the court that his family had gone down the river on a boat that had sunk after hitting a yellow-bellied catfish!

The Long Wait

Pittsburgh was the last chance for flatboat "captains" to shop for the supplies they would need on the trip ahead. They bought pumps for leaks, and many bought small sails, thinking the wind would help the boat move. Later, they would discover that the wind blew from the wrong direction almost every day, so the sails were useless except to cover a leaking cabin roof. A small skiff with a flat bottom was a good buy for $5. The skiff was handy for trips ashore to hunt or to visit a village.

No rules had been set up for boats to have lights at night, horns, life jackets, or any kind of safety equipment that boats must have today to travel the rivers. Few flatboat captains would have known what to do with a compass, and a chart of the river was unheard of.

The best buy of all was a book called *The Navigator,* sold in Pittsburgh for one dollar. Taking the place of a chart, it told the amateur boatmen where the dangerous places were and provided a running commentary on the countryside the boatmen were passing. Many a traveler was influenced to stay in a certain village because of what *The Navigator* had said about the area. The book was easy to read, in layman's language, and it numbered the islands all the way down the river. There was no guarantee, however, that the book's information was correct.

> Island No. 10, three miles below No. 9, is tolerably large, about one mile long, and lies nearest the left shore, the river turns to the right. At the head of No. 10 is an ugly sand bar; in low water you must hug the left shore pretty close around the bend, keeping both the bar and island to your right. In high water, the right pass may be gone [through], providing you hug the right-hand shore, keeping off the island; it is something nearer than the left channel. The pass between the bar and the island is extremely dangerous.

> NEW MADRID, 12 miles below No. 10. About 20 years ago, Col. George Morgan, formerly of New Jersey, now of Washington County, Pennsylvania, in company with several other gentlemen, laid out a town here on a large scale, which they called New Madrid. It contains but a few houses, and is situated on a beautiful tract of land on the right bank of the river in lat. 36°30′N.

Travelers found plenty to do while waiting for the river to start running. The men studied *The Navigator* and picked up travel information from the more experienced boaters. Women and children tried to make the boat livable, piling the supplies carefully so that the boat was balanced. They packed the foods so water leaking in from above or below would do as little damage as possible.

The inside of the flatboat or keelboat was usually one room

Arks carried several families at one time—but not always in comfort

that seemed large enough until the supplies and belongings were carried in. At one end was, sometimes, a brick chimney and fireplace just like those the family had left back home. If there was no fireplace, cooking was done on a "caboose," a box of sand with a stove set in it. Families used imagination in making their temporary homes comfortable. Grandmother's rocking chair was set before the fireplace, where the children played just as they had back home.

One keelboat family stacked their supplies in the stern and made a family room in the bow. Then they tied ropes across the boat and divided the rest of the space into a long hallway with several "bedrooms" opening from it. Walls were made by hanging sheets and curtains over the ropes.

Housewives used their last chance to buy supplies in the "Gateway" stores. Where they were heading, it might be many years before they could buy shoes and heavy clothing again. Items such as needles, tinware to cook in, thread, pen points, saleratus (like our baking powder), soap, candles, corn brooms, horseshoe nails, tea, and glassware might not be seen again. Even a few luxuries such as lace trimming were not passed up. After all, a young daughter would grow up and marry somewhere out west and what mother could resist laying aside a few pretty items for her daughter's hope chest?

The curious thing about shopping in Pittsburgh was the merchants' fondness for barter. The man who rode over the mountains on his eighty-dollar horse with hopes of selling it for cash found that Pittsburghers did not pay money for such things. They had horses. Instead, they asked him if he would like to trade his horse for some flour, salt, hogs, or land. Or maybe some cast-iron salt pans, Indian corn, a Dutch looking-glass.

This trading—instead of buying—was very hard on the small farmer who could not get money for his products but could only get "an order on the store" in exchange for what he had to sell. If the storekeeper was ruthless, he tried to convince the farmer to sit down in the store and "drink his order" before he left. The poor farmer whose children needed shoes was often told there were no shoes, but how about some very good liquor or a practically new German flute?

Many "tradesmen" who knew how the system worked earned their living by arriving in Pittsburgh with something wanted there—new shoes, a piano. They traded that for something wanted farther down the river—glass bottles, paper, or hemp. Those items they would then trade for something wanted down in Natchez or New Orleans. With the cash they received in New Orleans, they boarded a ship bound for the West Indies. There, they loaded up on items that would sell for cash in the seaports along the Atlantic Coast. Then they left for Pittsburgh and began the circle of trade all over again.

Stores in Pittsburgh carried "everything that could be expected to be asked for" from an anchor to a child's whistle. At the market house in the city square, beef was 3 cents a pound, veal 7 cents a pound, a haunch of venison 50 cents, and a flitch of bear was one dollar. Eggs cost 5 cents a dozen, butter 14 cents a pound, and milk 3 cents a quart. All the boat families stocked up.

The Wind Changes

Suddenly one day the wind came out of the southwest and the ice began moving downstream. Thousands of people who now lived along the edge of the river stepped up their activity. One night the level of the water rose ten feet before morning and the current was flowing fast. By daybreak, men were fastening animals, a plow, and parts of a dismantled wagon onto the flatboat roofs. The decks were cleared for the crew to move quickly from side to side. The chattering of children and housewives disappeared as they went inside. Some flatboat owners lashed their boats and the boats of other families together. They thought the larger bottom on the surface of the water would help them travel faster. The clumsy flatboats all pushed out into the river on the same day. Pittsburgh lost the whole "suburb" along its waterfront within a few hours. The long "holiday" had begun.

Not all the passengers were aware of the dangers the men worried about as they swept downstream on the spring floods. Sandbars and islands were continually shifting. Islands "moved" upstream because mud piled up on the upstream side and the water cut away the downstream side. An island moved several hundred feet in a few years this way. Driftwood on a sandbar or trees of a good size were the only indication that an island was a permanent one instead of a moving one.

When a boat grounded, everyone jumped off into the water to help push it off again. However, the ironclad rule of helping other boats in trouble did not always apply. There was still enough danger from river pirates that it was risky to help a complete stranger.

Flatboaters loved to tell the story of the French prince, Louis Philippe, who came to the New World with his brothers to travel through the west. When their keelboat landed on a bar, one of the crewmen hollered down into the cabin, "You kings down there. Show yourselves and help us pull off this bar."

Hidden Dangers

Although *The Navigator* was published every year and corrected often, there were some perils it could not keep up with. The river might open up a new route for itself overnight. An inattentive boatman could shoot through a cutoff, only to find his boat stuck in a little bayou with no way to get back into the main river current. Banks caved in, taking trees with them. The trees formed "wooden islands" or "rafts" of great size to lie in wait for the small boats careening down the river.

Often the heavy roots of a tree sank to the bottom, its top branches under the water but still pointing upward. The branches could easily puncture a hole in an oncoming boat. These were called "planters." Trees that bobbed up and down and could be seen were called "sawyers" or "snags." "Sleeping sawyers" hid just beneath the surface of the water to snag a passing hull.

A flatboat could sink in just a few minutes. One owner saved his sinking flatboat by throwing an armful of quilts overboard at the spot where his boat had been stoved in. Suction pulled the quilts into the hole, patching the boat just long enough for it to be poled into a shallow spot where the broken plank was repaired.

Sudden weather changes brought many a crisis to the boatman's day. Storms arrived unannounced, with winds heavy enough to push flatboats or keelboats onto bars. Seams ripped open and water poured in. Travelers who took off too early in the year discovered that chunks of ice could rip holes in the side of a boat as easily as rocks.

Travelers with the American mania for speed often continued on their way all night—at least while they were still on the relatively safe Ohio River. Very dark nights and thick fog often made it hard to tell how far a boat was from shore. One trick was to throw pieces of coal or stones to hear them bounce off trees on the shore. To find the channel where the

Travelers were impressed with the city of Cincinnati in 1802

water was deepest on a dark night, the boatman learned to dip water from each side of his boat. The resistance of the current told him which side had the deepest and fastest-running water.

River travelers had heard that they would find many differences between the settlers on the left bank of the Ohio and those on the right. On the north side, the Ohio farmers called Kentucky people "thieves." On the south side, Kentuckians warned travelers to watch out for "Yankee tricks" if they stopped on the Ohio shore. Occasionally boatmen stopped on both shores to hunt raccoon or quail. Many an unsuccessful hunt ended with the boat's passengers enjoying a fresh roast chicken for dinner—which is why both Ohioans and Kentuckians called flatboaters "chicken stealers."

River Traffic

All kinds of traffic followed the river—almost all of it going in the same direction. A traveler could buy a passage on an Ohio packet boat for $25 for a 500-mile trip, as John Force did in 1828. John had none of the worries of the flatboat owner and found it "a very pleasant voige." He described the boat as "a kind of wooden prison" with four rooms, each with an iron stove. The sleeping rooms had berths stacked along the walls, each six feet long and two feet wide. He had four meals each day, plus a tea party before going to sleep at night.

James Lambdin did not have as good luck on the keelboat for which he bought passage in May. There were forty passengers, he said, "all of whom, with the exception of myself and one other man, thought they were to be provided for on board." James had packed himself a basket of ham, cheese, crackers, and bread, expecting his food to last for a month-long trip. When the other passengers discovered there was no food on the keelboat, he had to share his basket. His month's supply of food was gone in one day. As night fell, the passengers also discovered there were no beds. They lay on boxes and bales of merchandise and slept fitfully. James got off the boat at the first stop downriver.

Some flatboats were fitted out as general stores. Approaching a built-up area, the captain blew a horn to announce his arrival. If there was no place to tie up near shore, his customers arrived by canoe. This floating shopkeeper had to barter because most of his patrons had no money.

Louisville, Kentucky, had traffic jams on the shore as well as in the river

Instead, they exchanged the products of their own farms—flour, cotton, tobacco, and wild-animal skins—for what they needed at the store. One flatboat was a floating flour mill. It moved down the river to serve towns that had no mills nearby. Another was a floating sawmill. Its owner found enough business to stay a week or two in each village.

Professional boatmen used keelboats instead of flatboats. Then, when they had gone as far down the river as they intended to go, they began the laborious trip back, poling "fernenst" the stream. Where the river was too deep for poling, the crews used a towline and pulled the boat as they walked along the shore. Often they had to wrap the line around one tree after another to keep the boat from slipping backward in the current. The trip downstream to New Orleans took six weeks. The return trip took four or five months. Travelers, however, did not go back upstream.

Special Sights

The river trip had landmarks the travelers could watch for. Not far from the "Gateway to the West," they watched for the place where the trees had been cut down to show the Ohio, Virginia (there was no West Virginia then), and Pennsylvania borders. Then came the town of Steubenville with its huge brick house in the wilderness. Wheeling was the very last place they could stop for supplies. The Muskingum River made the Ohio wide at the little town of Marietta—famous for building oceangoing sailing ships.

Somewhere farther west, each traveler found the place where he wanted to leave the river. Those headed for bluegrass country got off at Limestone, Kentucky. Those going to bear grass country left at Louisville. Those going toward Lake Erie headed up the Muskingum River. For John Force, the place to get off was Cincinnati.

"After miles of wilderness," he said, "I couldn't believe my eyes to see the number of people and waggons and saddlehorses and the quantities of meat, flour, corn, fish, fowls, and sauce of all kinds that were offered for sale!"

Eventually the boats that continued downstream reached the place called the Falls of the Ohio at Louisville. Of all the sights on the trip, this was the most dreaded. It was precisely because of these falls that flatboats and keelboats were not over fourteen feet wide. In two miles, the Ohio River plunged down twenty-two feet, churning over rocks and a shelf of limestone. When the river was running high, wide boats could pass easily enough. But when it was not very high, there was only one passage. It lay between two huge rocks that were only fifteen feet apart.

The Falls were so dangerous that the Kentucky state line, instead of running down the middle of the river at that point, was extended to include the opposite shore. This was so that all the pilots employed to guide boats down through the Falls were from Kentucky. Kentucky boatmen had the reputation of being "half horse, half alligator, and a little touch of snapping turtle." The price for a pilot was $2, whether the boat was a canoe or a 300-ton ship built in Marietta.

"At four miles distance, we could plainly hear the murmurings of the rapids, it being a calm, clear morning," said Peter Haward when he reached the Falls. "At seven, we came to the head of the Falls to take a pilot."

Twenty-five minutes later, Haward's big ungainly ark was safely below the rapids and he breathed a thankful sigh.

"The passage of the Falls is truly a magnificent scene. The rapidity with which we go and the increasing rolling of the water are terrifying."

From the Falls on, the northwest shore was called the Indian shore. But fear of Indians had not kept hundreds of travelers from scratching their names and initials at a place called Cave-in-the-Rock near Shawneetown. The cave, which even now commands an excellent view both up and down the Ohio River, was once the den of river pirates. By 1825, the cave walls had already been well filled with travelers' names.

The Big River

The moment of entering the Mississippi River was the high spot of the trip. It was also a place of quick decision-making for many people. Those who had thought they would turn north and go up the great river were struck dumb to see how huge and powerful it was. Its current ran three times as fast as the Ohio's. The channel was filled with debris, including huge trees that could pound a hole in a small boat with lightning speed. A flatboater or keelboater saw instantly that his little craft was safer floating in the same direction as that debris—at least it would not be hit quite so hard.

Now the boats really moved. They often made over forty miles in a day. Those who dared to travel at night made 95 miles in 24 hours. But there were so many snags to catch a small boat that night travel was only for the foolhardy.

The "Massasip" had its own special beauty. With a fishing line, a boatman could catch a catfish that weighed from 25

Rivergoing boats made sturdy homes

to 90 pounds. And there was no medicine in the world like its water.

"It scours your insides," said the boatmen. One fourth of it in a cup was mud. But not all travelers enjoyed drinking it. One man said, "If I have but a peck of dirt to eat in life, I know I shall get my share on this trip and forever after be exempt from it."

The downstream trip ended when the traveler reached the place where he wanted to stop. The trip had not been a holiday by any means, but it had been educational. There was also a fringe benefit the flatboat buyer had not thought of. Flatboats could be taken apart easily and turned into livable small cabins. Many old homes in New Orleans today claim flatboat parts. Some boats were sold for their wood and became wooden sidewalks or small outbuildings. Fort Washington in Cincinnati was made entirely from flatboats. Perhaps the travel book was right about the river trip being cheap—if the flatboater figured he had also bought himself a house for settling in the wilderness.

6

Four Miles an Hour by Covered Wagon

Moving Back

Everyone had a favorite means of travel to go all the way west. But there was only one means by which a man could take his family, his farm animals, a load of tools, and the furniture. That was by covered wagon.

The snow was still deep on the ground when Mary Eliza and John Warner told their friends at school about their trip in the spring. Mr. Warner raised horses in Iowa, and his brother Chester took them to California to sell. The day after Chester returned from the west, the family gathered to hear about the beautiful land of sunshine where he had sold the horses for so much money. The entire family decided to take the rest of the horses and go west to live.

"Only we are moving all the way back," John told his friends proudly.

"Moving back" was what everyone called going west. Most people who lived near the Mississippi River still thought that going east was "going home." Going west was moving back into unknown country.

Most travelers going far west bought light emigrant wagons. The huge Conestoga wagons that were used to haul freight in the east were used by traders on the Santa Fe trail in the southwest. But Conestoga wagons had to be pulled by six or eight horses or oxen. That cost too much for ordinary families.

The light emigrant wagon was the best way to go west with the family

Light emigrant wagons held a ton of goods and were pulled by only two or four animals. The wagons could be driven, and often were, by a woman with a baby on her lap. Over the top, a white canvas roof kept out most of the rain and trail dust. In the front and rear, the canvas pulled together tightly, leaving only a little round window to let in fresh air or give the inside passengers a view of the changing scenery.

The wagons were called "emigrant wagons" because the travelers in them really were emigrants. They actually left the United States borders to go west. After they crossed the uncharted Indian Territories they were back in the states once more, for California had become a state in 1850. However, travelers called every person an emigrant who traveled with his family to a new state.

A good wagon for the journey west was riveted, not bolted, together. The rough, rocky trails quickly shook apart wagons that were put together with nuts and bolts. The wheels were made of white oak or Osage orangewood because those woods did not shrink in dry desert country and so let the iron tires fall off. The wagon buyer also checked to see that the wagon bed fitted tightly all around so that water would not seep in when the wagon crossed streams.

After finding good wagons, the western traveler had to decide whether to have them pulled by mule, horse, or ox power. Mules were cheap until 1859, when they cost $100 each. They were good in hot country, but balky about pulling wagons. They had to be led, and no mule would round a strange corner on a trail unless it was following an animal it trusted.

Horses were not tough enough to pull heavy wagons, and their food was a constant problem. The dried grass on the prairies and dusty plains nourished the western horses, but a "states horse" would not touch it. Horses strayed at night if they were not hobbled—and if they were hobbled at night, they became useless after a few weeks. The greatest disadvantage of using horses, though, was that they attracted a great deal of attention from the Indians.

Indians were not interested in the slow, plodding oxen. Oxen ate whatever grass they could find along the path. They could be turned loose to graze and wouldn't stray far. They were tough and easy to control, never stampeding like

The inside of John Bemmerley's family wagon as it looked in 1849 going from Cincinnati, Ohio, to Yolo County, California

horses and cattle. But it was the price—about $25 each—that decided most travelers on ox power for their wagons.

Most families also took a few horses to use for scouting, hunting, and rounding up strays. Some even started the cross-country trip with the family carriage pulled by horses or mules. This gave the children and women another place to ride during the day. But eventually, most of the carriages shook to pieces on the trails.

What to Take

Western travelers learned to pack clothing made of tough, long-wearing material. Girls and women had two dresses each, both made of linsey-woolsey, a rough cloth of linen and wool. Men and boys had duck trousers or jeans. Both men and women wore the same kind of stout wood-pegged shoes or boots. No everyday women's shoes were tough enough to withstand a walk of more than ten miles. Each family member wore a tough felt hat for protection from the sun.

The family packed food for a variety of weather conditions. Bacon spoiled quickly in heat, so they put it in a wooden box and packed it with bran to keep it cool. Flour went in double sacks and sugar in India-rubber bags. Butter, which they made before leaving home, kept fairly well in tins that were soldered shut. They cut vegetables and fruits into thin slices, pressed them into cakes, and dried them until they were as solid as rocks. Later, when water was added, these "rocks" became mushy copies of the original. Each person needed 200 pounds of "breadstuff" (meaning flour and crackers). During the trip, on rainy days when no dry wood could be found to start a fire, crackers often made up the entire meal.

Lemonade was not for a treat, but was a necessity to keep the travelers from getting scurvy. A few drops of fresh lemon juice were added to citric acid, sugar, and water to make the refreshing drink. When the lemonade ran out, the children were sent scurrying to find wild onions, wild grapes, or dandelion greens. People had no idea why these foods prevented scurvy, because they had never heard of vitamins—they just knew these things worked. For special treats along the way, the women packed loose tea, maple sugar, hard cheese, vinegar, pickles, coffee, smoked beef, and cans of sardines.

One wagon was never enough for a family. Since most travelers planned to farm as soon as they reached their new homes, they needed wagons to carry farming tools, harnesses and plows, a grindstone, building tools, seeds to plant, and a crate of chickens. After gold was discovered, though, many of the travelers were going west to find fortunes without working. Every traveler had some kind of list of supplies such as this one for a medium-sized family in 1848:

rifles	buttons	beeswax and tallow for
pocket-	pins	greasing
knives	thimble	opodeldoc liniment for
whetstone	toothbrushes	animals
ax and awl	comb and	drinking cup for the family
hammer and	brush	chains to help go down
saw	castile soap	slopes
hatchet	shoeleather	cask to carry water across
shovel	shoe pegs	desert
gimlet	nails, tacks	bucket of tar
spyglass	scythes	herbs, medicine and doctor
lantern	ropes	book
scissors	goggles	washbowl and soap
twine,	horse-	green veils for sun and dust
thread	shoes	India-rubber water bottles
bar soap	palm and	cotton cloth to make
wool	pricker	curtains, clothes
mittens	to sew	candles and wax
Bible	canvas	lucifers

Leaving Home

At last the time came to leave home. Not all travelers going west went as far as California or Oregon. Some moved short distances—from Ohio to Illinois or through the Cumberland Gap into Kentucky.

"I wanted only to go to where the great prairies rolled away mile after mile," said Ephraim Banning. "To where the sky seemed to bend down to the earth . . . where none of its green had been turned back with a plow . . . or belittled by fences."

Families who traveled only a short way (a trip of 40 or 50 days) left home during the cold early months of the year. They wanted to arrive at their new homesite by April. They had to clear land, build a shelter, and be ready to plant by May.

Travelers like the Warner family, with a four-month trip ahead of them, planned to arrive at Independence or St. Joseph, Missouri, sometime in April. There they set up a camp with thousands of other people just like them. They waited on the edge of the prairies for the spring rains to end and the grass to start growing on the plains. Without grass for their animals to eat, they had no "fuel." One look around at the hordes of people all waiting to go to the same place at the same time showed them just how many animals would be needing that grass.

These last days of waiting had their excitements and upsets. Jane Gould felt she was leaving civilization forever. She went into the city with her children to have their miniatures (photographs) taken. But the day was cloudy and the photographer said he needed bright sun. Susan Magoffin, a bride of

The women had to cook before reaching the treeless prairies

eighteen, went into the city to fill her "plunder basket" with fruits, candy, and books. But Amelia Warner, the mother of Mary Eliza and John, had a problem of another sort on her mind.

All the ladies in her wagon train were wearing those curious new pants called "bloomers." They were worn underneath a dress so short it came to just below the knees. One of the women in the group had made fun of Amelia in her long dress—said she was proud and just wanted to look better than the others. Finally, Amelia went with her younger sister, Celia, into the woods where no one—not even her family—could see her. Each of them tried on a pair of the hated bloomers.

"We practiced with them," Amelia said. "Celia decided she had the courage to wear hers. I find I am brave enough to cross the plains, but not brave enough to wear bloomers . . . not as long as my two dresses last!"

Other waiting days were busy with homely chores. The women washed clothes in tubs and dried them by spreading them out on bushes. They cooked beans and rice in great quantities. Soon, when they reached the treeless prairies, they would not have enough fuel to make foods that took a long time to cook. They wrote letters to the folks at home to tell them how much fun it all was. Their families could send them mail at one of the forts or towns where the wagon train would be stopping.

The last important piece of business at the edge of civilization was to join a company. No one really wanted to travel across unknown territory alone. Families were safer in company with others. Besides, they could share the jobs and equipment. A company had anywhere from five to a hundred wagons. Smaller companies traveled faster and needed less grass for their animals at each stop. But larger companies offered more safety in Indian country.

The members of a company voted in new members and elected one man to be captain, usually someone who had made the trip at least once before. His word was law, just as if he had been the captain of a ship. He even decided what day the wagon train should leave the camping ground.

Moving Out

The wagon drivers drew numbers for their position in the train. The wagon that was at the head on the first day then moved to the last in line the following day. Each family had its turn to be the first wagon and the rest of the time to eat dust behind the others. The travelers were all impatient for their first sight of the prairies. The plains were flat and the

The travelers had never seen storms like those
on the plains

driving was very easy at first, giving everyone a feeling that
the trip would not be so bad after all.

Many young men on their first trip west were like Joe
Buffam, fresh out of college. Joe wrote in his diary that he
was on the prairie the day he arrived in Independence,
Missouri. That night, when he and his friends found a place
to sleep on a cabin floor, Joe said, "I suppose this is what it
will be like the whole way west." Actually, it was Joe's last
night with a roof over his head for several months. He began
to get the picture a few mornings after the company moved
out when he woke up with a rattlesnake curled beneath the
blanket he was using as a pillow.

The prairies did not begin until after the wagon train had
crossed the Missouri River. Just before starting across the
prairies, the company rested while the women cooked food
for the trip ahead. From here on, wood was to become

scarcer. By the time they reached Fort Kearney (now in Nebraska), the cattle were so happy to see trees that each animal rushed for its own tree and rubbed up against it.

Rainstorms on the prairies were guaranteed to build character. None of the travelers had ever seen vivid, forked lightning like that flashing across the flat prairie. Few travelers had ever seen so much sky all in one eyeful. They had lived in small towns or cities, where mountains, trees, or buildings blocked the view of approaching storms. Susan Magoffin spoke of her first storm like this:

"There was no object near that was higher than our wagons, and how easy it would have been for one of them to be struck. With it was a high wind—enough to counteract the effects of the drenching rain."

"For a rainy day breakfast," said Jane Gould, "we all crowded into the wagon . . . using the trunk for a table. I made some coffee and warmed the beans. Then I put the dishes under the wagon till 4 P.M. when the rain stopped and it was the first time I left the wagon."

Some travelers carried iron stoves in their wagons to use in their new homes. These were not used for cooking on the trip because there was never enough dry wood. Instead, the cooks dug a hole in the ground, built a fire, and sometimes used a reflector oven to bake bread, biscuits, and an occasional potato. Each person had a folding campstool to sit on. The table was made of two long boards covered with white oilcloth. Oilcloth was shiny on one side and smooth like plastic so it could be wiped clean. In wet weather, the same oilcloth doubled as a raincoat.

Occasionally there were special treats at mealtime. Fresh doughnuts, red and white currants covered with sugar, fresh onion soup made from onions grown by a ferryboatman, a blueberry pie made with berries the children had picked, or trout that the boys had caught in a river—all helped to keep up the travelers' spirits.

"Nooning" was the best time of day. The largest meal was eaten then, and some of the travelers caught up on sleep they had missed the night before. The animals had a chance to rest, nibble grass, and drink water. Children were sent off on excursions to find small kindling sticks. During the hottest part of the day, everyone was grateful for the rest that split the long day's journey in half.

Nooning was not so pleasant after the wagons reached the prairies. Then the only shade they could find was under the

Travelers pass through the city of Lecompton when it was the capital of Kansas Territory

wagons. Instead of searching for wood, everyone picked up buffalo chips—the droppings from buffaloes. The chips made a good fire unless they were wet. Unfortunately, they did add a certain unwelcome flavor to the coffee and food cooked over them. When the buffalo herds began to disappear from the prairies, this handy source of fuel disappeared with them.

On the long trip, the women filled their time knitting, crocheting, and helping their husbands to drive the teams. The women travelers were capable of doing all the work required of them and handling most of the men's jobs besides. Often a woman who was left a widow on the trail with little children to raise had no choice but to fill her husband's shoes. The women visited back and forth with other women in the same train, exchanging cooking ideas to pep up the dull everyday diet of beans, crackers, and rice. On walks, they filled their apron pockets with berries, currants, and nuts for dessert surprises.

Keeping the children in the wagons was all but impossible. They were all over—collecting spruce and pine gum to chew on, sliding down snow slides in the mountains, gathering small chips of wood to start fires. Older children helped care for the babies. Infants rode in baskets, which were sometimes strapped onto a wagon seat or hung on a packsaddle.

After dinner in the evenings, the men often had a "ball play." A fiddler played tunes for singing, but dancing waited until the wagon train arrived at a fort. Mothers washed out the towels used for diapers and dried rows of them in front of the campfire. When another company camped nearby, the ladies of one camp "went calling" on the ladies of the other. Those ladies then, very properly, "returned the call" within the next few days just as if they were all back home in the city.

Often there were serious arguments in a company. Troublesome people were voted out of the company. When one young man was voted out, he said, "We had a devil of a fuss and I left the camp and went with another company." There was always the chance that, when one company voted a person out, another company might refuse to let the outsider in.

The first exciting stop on the trail was Fort Kearney. In addition to seeing trees, which they had not seen for many days, the travelers saw new faces besides those which had become so familiar in their own company. Sometimes there were letters waiting from home, and there were always letters to be written and sent back east. The company fiddler played for a dance—the last occasion for a formal dance for many weeks.

Great Platte Highway

Fort Kearney marked the start of the superhighway to the west—the Great Platte River Road. It was not really a road at all—just a flat place alongside the Platte River where, today, part of Interstate 80 runs between Kearney and Ogallala. The riverside path climbed so gradually that the travelers hardly noticed. They were content just to walk in the shade of trees and have water near for themselves and their animals. At one point, the trail was so narrow between the river and a bluff that, if there were any Indians near, the travelers did not dare to use the trail, but climbed over the bluff instead.

Chimney Rock was in sight three weeks before
the travelers reached its base

Windlass Hill, near Ash Hollow, was so steep that the
wagon drivers had to lock their wheels so the wagons would
not go downhill faster than the oxen. On steep hills, the rear
wheels were locked and a piece of chain run under each for
traction. Often the oxen were hitched to the back of the
wagon to keep it from plunging down. The men wrapped
their guide ropes around trees to slow their wagons. Naturally, everyone was in all kinds of hurry.

"Great time going down a steep hill," said one boy.
"There were two hundred wagons at the top, all trying to
be first. It took two hours to go down."

One day the captain pointed out a strange sight in the
distance. It looked like a giant hand with a finger pointing
up.

"That's Chimney Rock," said the captain. The children
were so excited they didn't want to go to sleep for fear they
would miss seeing the rock up close. Every traveler wrote

A National Park ranger at Scott's Bluff shows a group of Boy Scouts the wagon ruts along the Oregon Trail

about Chimney Rock in his diary—not because it was so unusual or beautiful, but because it was three weeks after sighting it before they reached it.

Approaching Chimney Rock, the travelers passed near another pair of huge rocks that they nicknamed Courthouse Rock and Jail. All these sites were places to write a name and date, and the names can still be seen today. Now the path became steeper and the trains moved more slowly. On the other side of Chimney Rock, which looked, up close, like a tall monument on a giant haystack, was another strange formation. From a distance it looked like an ancient walled city. On Scott's Bluff, where the trail led through Mitchell Pass, one can still see today the wagon ruts that were made by these travelers.

After Scott's Bluff was the first encounter with alkali water —deadly for animals and none too pleasant for humans. Mothers bathed their children with glycerine water rather than use any of the alkali water on their skin. Many of the women complained that they looked like squaws. The red alkali dust had darkened their skins, but only temporarily. The dust choked their pores, found its way into the baggage, and made noses and lips very sore. For the next forty miles after the alkali water, travelers passed piles of ox bones. Every animal that had drunk the water had died.

Buffalo bones, and some of the other bones along the road, were used as a sort of newspaper. The travelers wrote messages on them and then dropped them in the path of the next wagon train for someone to read.

"The Miller family of Chillicothe passed this point the afternoon of August 3." "Indians rumored five miles northeast of here." "Poison water half mile south."

Fort Laramie was a welcome sight for many reasons. After

days of worrying about Indians and hearing distant drums, the travelers were happy to see the army troops and the comparative safety of a little log fort and stockade. More than 50,000 people went through Fort Laramie in 1850. Only a few years before, travelers had been a rarity. Now the merchants in the fort were planning to get their share of the money. A cup of sugar cost $2. A nickel plug of tobacco was $1.50. Bullets were 75 cents a pound and a 25-cent shirt cost $4. A coarse pair of pants brought $10. Later, when there was some competition, prices came down.

Beyond Fort Laramie was Register Cliff, rising a hundred feet straight up from the prairie. Thousands of travelers wrote their names and where they came from on the cliff face. Now almost every day brought new landmarks and sights—cactus, a natural bridge, strange-looking rocks. Ahead in the distance were the mountains that marked the Continental Divide. The path left the North Platte River soon afterward.

Halfway There

Halfway between Missouri and California was a long flat, high chunk of solid rock called Independence Rock. When there were no Indians to worry about, everyone climbed up to its flat top for a view of the valley. The rock came to be called "the bulletin board of the Sweetwater Valley," because names and messages were all over it. Mary Warner's family found a special place to write their names, however.

"On one side is a small cave," said Mary. "We left our names there. I told my husband if we got killed by Indians, there at least would be our stone and epitaph."

The Fourth of July was a very special occasion for those on the plains just as it was for Americans anywhere else. Independence Rock was named by travelers who had reached it on The Fourth. No matter where a wagon train was on that day, the celebration included singing, dancing, and fun. Since they had no fireworks, the travelers fired their rifles all day long—which must have been a puzzlement to any Indians in the area.

"On Independence Day, I went to another company a mile distant," said one young man. "Found a fiddler and had a dance on the green. And also had some of the 'oh-be-joyful.' "

Drinking was rare in the wagon trains. Most wagons had no space to carry liquor except what was necessary for medicine. Every man was needed in a company, and no captain could tolerate a man who was not alert—even in his sleep. Besides, with the women and children along, the men had little chance for a nip of the "oh-be-joyful."

Traveling west through South Pass, the wagons at last crossed the Continental Divide. It was the one place where covered wagons could pass over the backbone of the Rocky Mountains on an easy grade. From this point on, all water flowed toward the Pacific Ocean. At a place called Pacific Springs, everyone celebrated with a taste of the water. But the trip was far from over.

Sometimes the trails went for miles over rocks of all sizes, making it impossible for anyone to ride inside a wagon. A sudden down drop of a wagon broke an axle. If the wagon turned too sharply, the wagon tongue broke. Always the repairs had to be done at once on the road. In some places the road was so terrible that the company moved only half a mile all day.

The wagon trains often had to "noon" where there was no water. Then the animals had to be forced to move on. Oxen and mules remembered where they had last seen water and were very apt to turn around and start heading in the other direction at such a trot they could not be stopped. They also could smell water ahead. One day, when the animals had been a day and a half without food or water, they suddenly began to tread briskly. Then they broke into a run. They had smelled a river ahead. On another hot July day, the Gould family had traveled all day on a treeless prairie without water.

"The cattle were very thirsty and so were we," said John Gould. "Very little water was left in the can. A man told us there was a spring a mile and a half ahead on the road. It seemed a very long mile to us. When we got there, we found twenty or thirty teams ahead of us getting water from two very small springs. It took a long time to fill our cans."

Restless young people often wandered off the trail to sight-see or to climb a hill and look ahead. One day, Mary Eliza Warner (who was fifteen) and her young Aunt Celia climbed the hill ahead of the train to make some sketches.

"We went down into a ravine and took a cutoff," said Mary Eliza. "We were a good ways from the train. Then we saw fresh tracks of Indian ponies. [Indian ponies had no horseshoes] So we took the nearest route to the road. It was over a steep hill, but we made quick time climbing it."

The main reason for wandering away from the wagon train, however, was to answer a call of nature. There were no bathrooms or "necessaries" along the trail, except for a chamberpot kept inside the jolting wagon. The drivers had a hard time keeping track of who was in the wagons and who was walking along behind somewhere. One time little Annie

McMillan had lagged behind. The train had crossed a creek before someone shouted that Annie was missing. They knew she was too small to wade across the deep creek, so two men raced back to find her. One man was thrown by his mule into the creek and, although he wasn't hurt, he did lose his hat.

"Which is no trifling matter here!" he said angrily. Luckily, the men found Annie, and Annie's father gave the man another hat.

Watery Crossings

Usually the trail led the wagons to a place where streams and rivers could be forded. Often the same creek had to be crossed a dozen times in ten miles. But sometimes rivers had been swollen by rains and were too deep to cross. Where the deepest part was fairly narrow, the oxen could sometimes be hitched so that when the first pair of oxen was afloat, the second pair still had their feet on the stream bottom. Then by the time the first pair reached bottom on the opposite side, the second pair were afloat and a third pair were just entering the stream.

Usually the wagon bed (the bottom of the wagon box) was raised on blocks to help keep it out of the water on a crossing. In spite of everything, the food in the wagons got wet and sugar and coffee dissolved. Mary Warner's team got stuck in the middle of the river one day. Mary could not swim, but the sort of person who panicked in this situation never left home in the first place. Mary sat for six hours waiting to be rescued. She spent the whole time tatting a lace collar for her Sunday dress.

One way to get rich quick in the 1850's (easier than digging for gold) was to find a deep river, which wagons could not ford easily, and build a ferryboat. Anything that floated would do for a boat. One man tied together three dugout canoes made of hollowed-out logs. Then he waited for the customers to come down the trail. A wagon train captain then asked how much it would cost to use this homemade ferryboat.

"You buy the boat for $30," answered the ferryboatman. "Swim your cattle across. Then sell the boat for $30 to the next wagon train."

Usually the wagon train captain had to pay the money, but did not have time to wait for the next wagon train to come along the trail. This left the ferryboat owner with his boat to sell again and again.

Other ferryboatmen just charged outrageous tolls. One wagon train arrived at the Green River, still angry about the $5 per wagon bridge toll they had paid several miles back. When they reached the ferry, the captain asked how much it cost.

"Four dollars a wagon," answered the ferryboatman. "Swim your own cattle. And you'll have to wait two days for your turn."

The men of the company were furious. They had 43 wagons. They decided to build their own raft. After it was finished, they found they had no rope strong enough to work the raft across, because the Green River current was so swift and deep. They lost a good many of their ropes trying to make it work. The men of another company had tried turning their wagons bottom up. Then they put their empty water casks underneath to make the wagons buoyant. That didn't work either.

The captain of the 43-wagon company thought of another

idea. After looking over all the wagons, he selected two that could be caulked so their seams would not leak. They were to be used as boats. The men gathered up all the resin and tar they could find in the other wagons and worked until midnight caulking the two wagon boxes. The next day, the company unloaded all the wagons, took them apart, loaded

A wet part of the Great Platte River highway

the pieces and their belongings onto the two "boats" and floated them across the stream. On the other side, they put the wagons together again and repacked their possessions. It took two days for the whole train to get across. Meanwhile, four of their horses and a mule were stolen when they weren't looking.

Danger Ahead

The greatest danger facing the western travelers was not Indians—but sickness. Huge crowds of people headed west for gold in 1849. Cholera appeared in the dirty camps where wagon trains stopped for the night. No one had any idea what caused cholera. Some thought it was the beans and one company threw away every bean they had. Other people wore cotton stuffed in their ears and noses, trying to keep the germs in the air from getting inside them. The disease was so powerful that many people who were healthy in the morning were dead before night.

In addition to disease, an unusual number of deaths came from drowning in the rushing streams and from gunshot. And not always from Indian guns. One man, who wanted to remain nameless, told how one such accident happened.

"On June 4, 1854, four of us started out from camp to hunt for cattle that had strayed during the night. We were un-armed because we intended to go only a half mile from camp. Then we saw two men following us from camp. We thought it would be funny to scare the two. So we got down on all fours and growled. Bang with a rifle. Down went one of our men . . . the two supposing us to be wolves. He died in about twenty minutes. So much for fun on the plains."

The next day, he added this to his diary: "We buried Mr. Allan next morning as decently as circumstances would admit and started on our journey."

Hundreds of graves lined the trail—some marked with crosses and some with just a wagon tire iron. When a person died, the body was wrapped in a sheet. A tiny child was buried in a wooden cracker box—if one could be found. But

Rebecca Winters' grave was marked only with
a tire iron until her descendants added the
stone in 1902

there was no wood to spare for an adult coffin. Boards were
placed over the body in the grave and rocks piled on top of
the boards. Then the corral for the horses and cattle was
placed over the top of the grave. The animals trampled
down the grave site and their assorted smells kept wolves
from finding the grave and digging it up after the wagons
moved on.

"Then," said Jane Gould, "there was only a lonely grave

marker. No one to plant a flower or shed a tear."

Western travelers worried most about Indians. But for every murdering Indian, the travelers met up with several friendly ones. That did not make the Warner family any more confident the June night they were camped in Willow Springs. All day, Mary Warner had been worrying about the drumbeats she heard.

"Every thing I see in the distance, I think are droves of Indians," she said.

Suddenly, at one o'clock in the morning, the Warner company was awakened by the wild sound of eighty horses stampeding away from the camp. The men leaped from their beds. They wasted no time dressing but dashed out barefoot after the valuable horses. Three hours later, they returned with bleeding feet and no horses.

They just took time for some hot coffee, to put on their shoes and find warmer clothes. This time they saddled up what few horses were left in camp and took their guns. The women overheard the men agreeing that Indians had stampeded the horses. Mary and the other women and children burned everything they could spare to keep the fire blazing brightly.

"Imagine, if you can, our feelings," Mary wrote in her journal while she and the others waited for the men to return. That same fire they were keeping so bright for their men to return to was also being watched by the Indians out there in the darkness.

"There is one thing I learned," said Mary later. "You can get to the top of being frightened and then, in a measure, get over it."

The travelers found many Indians friendly and even likable. Women had a hard time to keep from admiring them.

On the other side of the desert—an exhausted
but happy family relaxes

Several women confided their feelings only to their diaries.

"He was real good looking—for an Indian."

Often it was the Indians who gave the people in the
wagon trains a tasty change from their ordinary dull diet,
bringing them fresh antelope meat which tasted like young
lamb.

"Antelope are too fast for our guns," one traveler re-
marked after an Indian gave him an antelope shot with bow
and arrow.

Indians visited the wagon trains to swap moccasins and
lariats for money, gunpowder, and whiskey. Their curiosity
and their naked little children annoyed the prim ladies of
the company. And there was still that fear.

"A good looking Indian came up to my buggy," said Mary Warner a few days after her experience at Willow Springs had ended with the safe return of most of their horses. "He wanted to shake hands. Well, of course I shook hands—and shook otherwise, too."

One Indian offered to trade three ponies for Mary's sister-in-law, Lizzie Warner. Her husband, a great practical joker, pretended to agree to the bargain until Lizzie was next to hysterical.

Terrifying deserts lay ahead of the travelers. At their edge, the wagon train stopped to get ready for the crossing. Men gathered buckets of the last grass they would see to feed their animals. The amount of grass they found depended on how many other wagon trains just ahead of them had done the same thing. They soaked the wooden wheels of the wagons in water. By now, the dryness of the road had shrunk the wood, so that many of the iron tires that bound the rims of the wheels no longer fitted and would not stay on. The wooden wheels swelled in the water, so the tires fitted again—for a while. The travelers soaked the bottoms of their shoes for the same reason—so the wooden pegs would swell and fit tight, holding the soles to the upper parts of the shoes. The women made bread pie to eat on the way.

After sunset, the company started across the sand. No road or signposts were needed. The road was littered with wagon irons, keg hoops (the wood had been used for fuel), piles of animal bones, and everything imaginable that had been too heavy for the fast dash across the desert. Sometime after midnight, the wagon train stopped so the travelers could build a fire for warmth and eat the bread pie. Then they hurried on so as not to be caught in the desert when the sun came up.

Destination

Crossing the mountains, the travelers found fields of wild flowers—from poppies and larkspur to sunflowers and primroses. Snow on the mountains in the middle of July and August delighted them. The Rockies and Sierras were more than five times as high as the Allegheny Mountains—and the travelers had thought those mountains were forbidding. For one man, it was the Green Mountains he found dangerous.

"Crossed the Green Mountains," he wrote in his diary. "A man would have to be very green to try crossing *them* a second time!"

Susan Magoffin, the young bride who headed down the Santa Fe trail on her honeymoon, was nearing her destination as well. Her train was heading for the mountains around Santa Fe, which was still a part of Mexico in 1846.

"We have passed 'The Vegas,' " said Susan. She had just met her first Mexicans that day and was shocked because the women had bare arms and necks. In fact, she said, their skirts covered little more than the calves of their legs. And when they crossed a stream, they pulled their skirts clear up to their knees!

The Mexicans no doubt found Susan strange, too, but they made friends by showing her their babies.

"The older women," Susan reported, "were clad in chem-

The pass through the Sierra Nevadas was 8,000 feet high, but on the other side was California gold

ises and petticoats only. And their rebozos [shawls]. Some of them had babies under their rebozos. I shant say at what business. I may venture this much though—that the little things were taking care of Number One."

There was a different feeling in the wagon trains as they approached the border of California. By now, the travelers had passed through all kinds of dangers and survived. There was a general feeling now that they might make it. And a great desire to have the long, long journey over.

Jane Gould found it very hard to be a good sport one day when the captain of their company decided to take another road.

"The captain decided to go the mountain road down the Humboldt instead of the bottom road," she groaned. "It was very rocky. Oh dear, I do so want to get there. It is now almost four months since we have slept in a house."

Jane was lucky the captain took the rocky mountain road. Others who took the river road found it to be some of the most desolate country of all. In places the red dust was like fine flour—eight inches thick on the road. The slightest movement raised the dust into their faces, filled their ears and noses, sifted through their clothing. The drivers could not see ten feet ahead. The alkali dust blistered their skin and lips and dried out their hair. One lady summed it up this way:

"It was worse than Indians, mosquitoes, storms, winds and even wood ticks."

Along the Carson River was "Rag Town." There the townspeople sold hay at an outrageous 25 cents a pound and water for 5 cents a gallon to the weary travelers. The town was depressing to those who had heard glowing tales of the "golden west." All the houses, including their roofs, were made of canvas nailed to posts in the ground.

Ragged as the town looked, it marked the edge of the very last mountain barrier the wagon train had to face. Even though the pass ahead was 8,000 feet high, there was no longer any holding back. California began at the mountains. The long trip was almost over.

7

SAILING THE COAST TO CALIFORNIA

Coastal Trips

Sailing was one of the pleasantest ways to get from one seaport city to another. There was no mud, no changing of horses, no broken axles, no taverns with bedbugs, and no crotchety wagon drivers. Most people felt safe knowing that coastal sailing ships were never very far out at sea.

Schooners, sloops, and brigs sailed on any water deep enough to float a ship—up rivers, across the Great Lakes, into Chesapeake Bay from the Delaware River through one of the earliest canals built in the country.

One day Henry McRoberts boarded a schooner to go to Newport, Rhode Island. The trip had barely begun when the anchor was lowered and the captain told the passengers there would be a delay of several hours. Many went ashore to sight-see. Others lounged on the deck, playing cards or writing a description of the place in their journals.

"There are winding rocks on both sides of the river," said Henry. "A vast current there is so agitated by different reefs of rocks that it forms a dangerous whirlpool. Boats that try to go through at the improper time of the tide or without a skillful pilot can be caught, whirled around and around and are dashed against the rocks."

The whirlpool that McRoberts described was not in some isolated part of the world, but in the East River near New York City. "Hell's Gates," as it was called then, is found on most maps of New York City today, underneath the Triborough Bridge. The treacherous whirlpool was tamed by dynamite over a hundred years ago. As sailing became safer close to shore, travelers who wanted an easier way to go west began thinking of sailing there.

Venturing Farther

The grandest trip of all was "around the Horn" to California. By sea, San Francisco was 15,000 miles from New York —five times the distance by covered wagon. The trip lasted the same length of time, about five months, and cost $250 for each person. The fringe benefits of sailing convinced many travelers that it was the best way to go.

There would be no Indians to worry about. A sea voyage was always good for one's health. And there would be no struggles with wagons and oxen across the terrible mountain ranges that were reported to lie somewhere between the prairies and California. Some maps called these mountains the "Northern Andes." British maps labeled them "The Stonies." Indian scouts called them "The Rockies." Whatever the name, everyone knew they were so high they made the Alleghenies look like a mere ripple in comparison.

The only danger, said most travelers whose information came from guess rather than experience, was shipwreck and

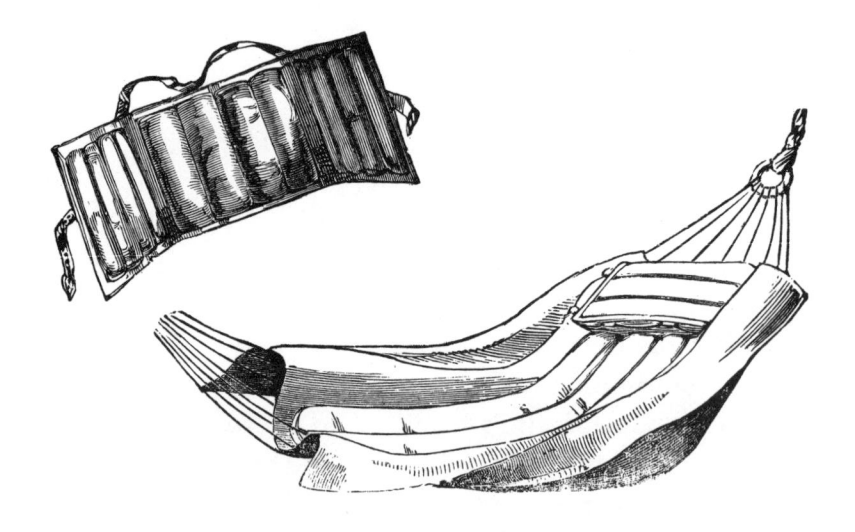

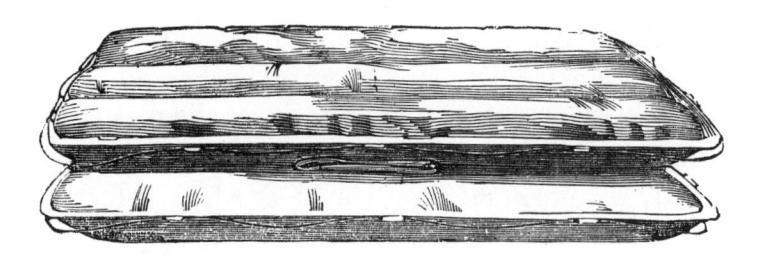

Many kinds of life preservers had been designed on paper, but none were guaranteed to work

drowning. To meet that risk, they made cork life preservers and floating beds for themselves and their families. Some people were embarrassed to board a ship with lifesaving equipment tucked under their arms, so they disguised it. One lady used her old feather boa—a fluffy neckpiece worn with afternoon dresses. She took out the wool lining, filled the inside with finely chopped up cork, and sewed it together again. If the ship sank, she had only to tie the boa tightly to her body with ribbons and float to safety. A gentleman who wanted to feel safe in stormy weather without giving the appearance of being scared pea green lined his vest with cork. Others designed folding mattresses for sleeping during the voyage that would become instant boats in case of emergency. The result was an unusual collection of life preservers, none of which would have supported a pet cat more than a few hours. But they gave sea travelers perfect confidence on shipboard.

Many travelers also took the advice of an early travel guide and learned to swim. Here was the swimming lesson in full:

> Choosing a place where the water deepens gradually, walk coolly into it until it is up to your breast. Then turn round your face to the shore and throw an egg into the water between you and the shore. It will sink to the bottom and be easily seen there if the water is clean. It must lie in the water so deep that you cannot reach to take it up, but by diving for it.

The swimming instructions reminded the timid beginner that he would then be facing toward shallow water. At any time, he could bring his legs under him and stand on the bottom so that his head would come up out of the water. The writer, who must have had very weak eyelids or else had never tried out his own advice, finished the lesson with these instructions:

> Then, plunge under the water with your eyes *open*— which must be kept open before going under, as you *cannot* open the eyelids for the weight of the water above you. Throw yourself toward the egg and endeavor, by the action of your hands and feet against the water, to get forward, till within reach of the egg. . . . You will then acquire the power of swimming naturally.

Sea Legs

With the fear of drowning gone, travelers turned their attention to packing enough clothing, treats, and seasick remedies to last for a voyage of five or six months. Since no one had been known to die of seasickness, the travelers claimed not to worry about it much. But many people confided their misery to their diaries—wailing, "Why don't sailors get sick on land like we get sick on the sea?"

One man decided that the way to beat seasickness was to keep eating. No sooner had he sat down to his soup than he groaned, "Oh Lord! Me and my dinner's going to have a fight certain!" The other people at his table laughed heartily as he disappeared after every course. Each time, he came tearing back to the table again and shouted, "Steward . . . some of the beef . . . quick!"

Not even sailors were immune to seasickness. Richard Henry Dana had just turned nineteen when he sailed on a brig to California in 1834. A bout with the measles had left him with such weak eyes that his doctor said he could not return to school. Instead, the doctor suggested a sea voyage to improve his health. Richard signed on the ship as a common sailor. Two days out of port, he wished he were dead. Finally a black man who was the ship's cook took pity on him.

"Now, my lad," he said soothingly, after Richard had lost all his meals to the fish, "you are well cleaned out. You haven't got a drop of your 'longshore swash aboard of you. You must begin on a new tack. Pitch all your sweetmeats overboard and turn-to upon good hearty salt-beef and bread, and I'll promise you, you'll have your ribs well sheathed and be as hearty as any of 'em afore you are up to the Horn."

Before long, every passenger could keep on his feet, even when the deck tilted in every possible direction. On ships that did not have cargo stored on deck, there was room for the passengers to take walks. Many read books, played cards, chess, or backgammon, or sketched shipboard scenes. A favorite game was Court Trials. Both sides of a court argument were represented by "lawyers" who argued fiercely for their clients. The sillier the argument, the better. One trial was the case of a man who had bitten another man. The biter was tried on a charge of cannibalism. A jury of twelve passengers decided which lawyer argued best.

Fun at Sea

Any day could be declared a special day and thus be eligible for some sort of special entertainment. The day a ship crossed the equator was marked with much ceremony by the passengers. King Neptune arrived on deck and initiated any person who had never before crossed the equator. On a ship without passengers, the ceremony consisted of the veteran sailors teasing some young sailor on his first voyage. On one ship, the sailors told the boy he must stay up on the forecastle as they neared the equator, so he could "catch a glimpse of the Line." They warned him that unless he kept his head down, he would be knocked overboard by the Line that went around the middle of the earth.

The Fourth of July was an occasion for celebration no matter where the American traveler might be. The cabin passengers often planned a special program and invited the passengers who were "between decks." On the brig *Andalusia,* there were speeches and music. One passenger read the entire Declaration of Independence aloud. A ship's band, consisting of whatever instruments and players could be found among the passengers, played stirring marches for a parade around the decks. On this particular occasion, the band consisted of three violins, a flute, a guitar, and one tambourine. The cook made soup from a pig's head and baked a real apple pie. For dinner there was chicken, beef, pork, pickles, hominy, rice, cranberry tarts, hash, and green peas. The captain shot off a cannon and every passenger who owned a gun fired it several times.

Many weeks later, the passengers of the *Andalusia* met the passengers from another ship. They compared notes on how they had spent The Fourth and those from the *Andalusia* were scandalized to hear that the captain of the other ship had not allowed his passengers to celebrate.

"Americans sailing on a ship who are not allowed to burn powder on the anniversary of Independence!" they gasped in horror. "It's unbelievable!"

In spite of the many amusements, most days on board ship were dull, with nothing better to watch than the porpoises. The *Andalusia* carried several people who were heading for California, where they all expected to get very rich digging gold. One lady kept herself occupied during the dull days by hemstitching handkerchiefs for her husband and his friends, until one misguided man made a remark.

"Women are lucky, because they have something to do like sewing during these long days," he said.

Immediately the lady told her husband that he should tell his friends she did not enjoy sewing and hereafter she would hem handkerchiefs only "at California prices."

Uncommon Days

As usual on a sea voyage, almost any occasion was good for a bet—when they would arrive at the Horn, whether they would go through the Straits of Magellan or around the Horn, what day they would cross the equator going north. A meeting with another ship invariably resulted in a race. Both crews and passengers shouted advice across the water:

"Better send your letters on our ship—as we will be there two weeks before you."

"Persons on land cannot judge what are the sensations of those at sea when meeting a vessel and exchanging salutations," said Ann Willson Booth, a passenger on the *Andalusia*. Here were people out of touch with the world just like themselves—and it was instant friendship.

When a ship approached from the opposite direction, the captain hoisted his special flag. Both ships backed their sails until they slowed to a stop. The first mate collected letters in a pillowcase and rowed to the other ship. When he returned, he carried news, sometimes newspapers or fresh fruit from a ship that had recently left a tropical port.

When they overtook a ship going in the same direction, the passengers leaned over the railings trading information as long as the two were within shouting distance. Sometimes they joined in singing songs, with their ships' bands playing a reasonable facsimile of the tune. One day, the *Andalusia* spoke a ship just coming out of Buenos Aires. Its captain asked why the *Andalusia* had so many people on board. He could hardly believe his ears when he heard they were all headed for California to dig for gold. He had not heard of the discovery of gold.

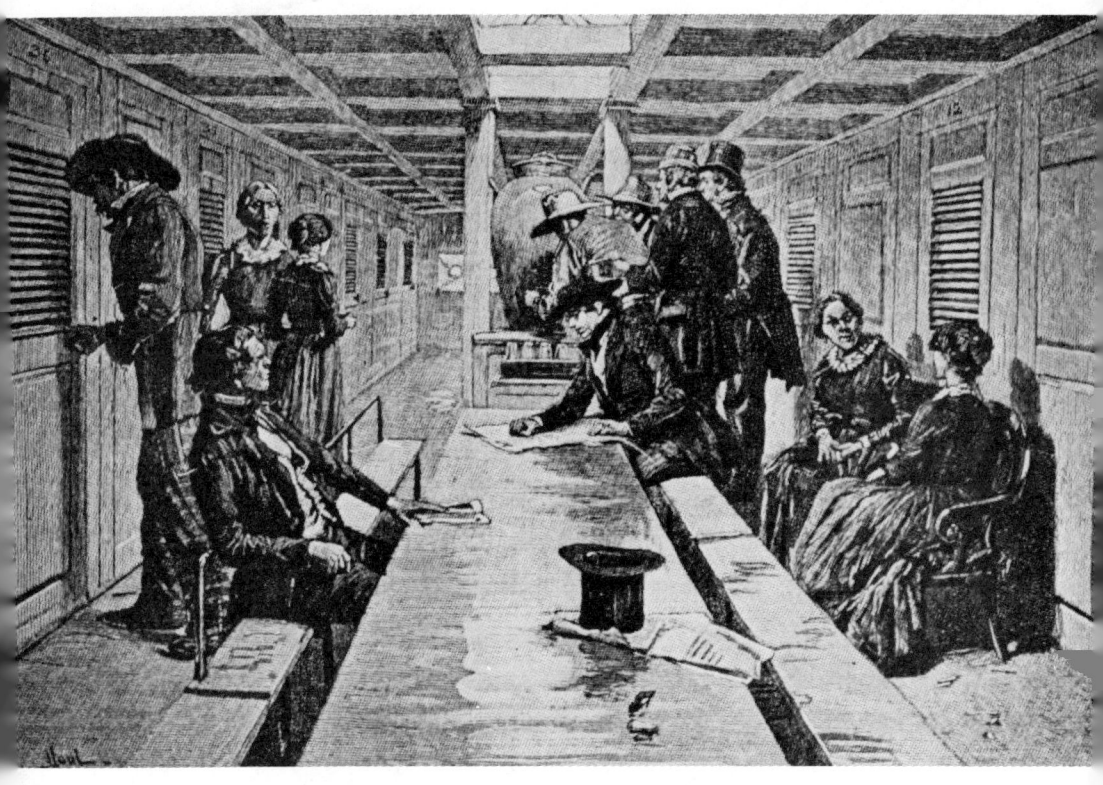

The dining saloon on a sailing packet to California

Some meals were good—some were terrible. Occasionally the dinner included some strange-looking fish that a sailor had caught in tropical waters. When the cook wondered whether or not the odd fish was poisonous, he tossed a sterling-silver button in with the fish. If the button turned black, he threw the fish away.

Above decks, there were occasional treats like jam or pickles that passengers had brought along. On the *Andalusia,* when the ship's goat died after a few weeks at sea, the passengers had no more cream for their coffee until the ship rounded the Horn and stopped in Chile so they could buy another goat. The between decks passengers ate sauerkraut twice a week and a great deal of salted beef. They sat at four long tables with a ship's officer at each table to see that "morality and cleanliness were observed."

"There is no Sunday off soundings," said a sailor, "and none *on,* if there's work to be done." Off soundings was where the ocean floor was too deep to be measured by a lead line. But on the *Andalusia,* there were Sundays.

A minister, Mr. Taylor, was one of the passengers. The first Sunday morning at sea, Mr. Taylor built a pulpit on the main deck and announced the hours of the services. The captain's niece, also a passenger, said she guessed the captain had never in his life been so near a pulpit before.

With church services scheduled for morning, afternoon, and evening on Sundays, the passengers and even the crew began to dress neatly. The sailors laid canvas over the rough benches to make clean pews. Mr. Taylor had brought along a supply of hymnals and spent most of the week writing his sermons. Unfortunately, his sermons were not interesting enough to keep the passengers' minds from wandering when there was anything more exciting around—such as an albatross, porpoises, or a ship.

One Sunday several ships came in sight while Mr. Taylor was preaching. Every head that dared to turn made him more angry.

"As soon as the preaching was over," said Ann Booth, "there was quite a general rush to the side of the ship to see the sails which by now were quite near."

Mr. Taylor was not so easily diverted from his path of saving their souls. One sin that worried him especially was their dancing. Each time the passengers had a dance to the music of their homemade band, Mr. Taylor and his wife walked across the dance floor, back and forth, until the dancers had to stop. The Taylors made more enemies than converts.

The Weather Eye

On ordinary days, the passengers wore their old clothes, spotted with food that had spilled on them when the sea was rough. The men wore no vests, coats, or suspenders on hot days. Their shirts were colored or checked. Sometimes they even went barelegged and barefooted. The ladies had no such luxury in warm weather.

The weather came in all varieties. Some days the sea was so calm that the passengers almost forgot they were on an ocean. On such a day, the ship did well to travel fifteen miles. Other days, the wind might change so suddenly in direction that the sails backwinded and pushed hard against the masts. The sailors had to act quickly before a mast snapped from the pressure.

The ship meandered slowly until it reached the southern trade winds. Then suddenly, one day, all would change. Every sail filled with a fresh breeze. The ship now traveled as much as 240 miles in a day. The chants of the sailors as they hauled on the ropes fascinated the passengers and so did the language.

"Haul the maincrotchicdown!" Ann Booth wrote in her diary, meant the ship was about to turn. Later, she changed it to read, "Haul the main crossjack down."

"Why should it rain so hard at sea?" one passenger moaned. "After all, there are no crops to raise, no dust to lay."

Sometimes the rains came in torrents. No passenger could step out on deck without an India-rubber suit. All hands were busy catching rainwater in canvas sails when it rained hard. Later, the passengers were allowed to wash their clothes in the extra water. Sometimes, though, the rainwater they caught had to be used for drinking water. One day on the *Andalusia,* the crew trapped 1,000 gallons. The passengers complained that it tasted like smoke because it had passed through the tarred rigging.

Then there were the storms. At first the passengers were amused.

"Amid the roaring of the sea and the shouting of the captain, together with the creaking of the masts and 'yo heave ho' of the sailors, we had quite a noisy time," said Ann Booth.

The passengers never knew what would happen next in a big storm. Crashes sounded all around at dinner as plates landed in laps. A settee turned over during a meal, sending two men head over heels with soup all over them. Everything not lashed down went whooshing off to the other side of the ship as it heeled over. Waves thumped unmercifully against the sides and dashed over the top of the cabin so that it seemed the roof would be broken in.

"I was compelled to hold on in bed with all my might," said one passenger. "And when the ship gave a heavy lurch —which was every five minutes—I was completely raised up above the board that was supposed to hold me in my bed."

Rounding the Horn

"I was wondering," said the captain, "whether the passengers would round the Horn without seeing the elephant."

"Seeing the elephant" was a favorite expression around the 1850's, with travelers at sea as well as on land. The term meant many things—to see the world and, in some cases, to have great expectations and be disappointed. Sometimes it meant to see more than you had bargained for. No one who sailed around the Horn to California missed seeing the elephant.

The passengers knew when the ship was nearing Cape Horn. On clear nights, they had been watching the Southern Cross in the sky. By day, they saw the Magellanic Clouds ahead in the southwest. Now the sky began to grow darker much earlier in the day. The weather was colder and the captain had to put a stove in the cabin, even though it was mid-July. For some weeks, the sailors had been making extra ropes and mending old sails for use if needed. They made it obvious that in rounding the Horn, one must expect the unexpected.

Ever since the voyage had begun, the passengers had dreaded approaching the Horn. Suddenly one day the sky grew a dark slate color. The sea ran higher with each succeeding wave. Nothing inside or outside the ship was dry. Hail and sleet fell so hard that the sailors could hardly perform their jobs in the rigging. The forward part of the ship dipped into the sea. When it rose again, a good bit of the sea came with it, hurling mighty waves down the deck.

"Here comes Cape Horn!" the captain shouted.

Will we go around Cape Horn? Or will the captain save

1,000 miles and go through the Straits? The question was good enough for another bet. When the moment of decision came, the captain looked to the winds. The *Andalusia* went around the Horn. Later, its passengers learned that a bark, the *Hebe,* had gone through the Straits. Contrary to what the *Hebe*'s captain had expected inside, the sea in the Straits suddenly became dead calm. Nine of the *Hebe*'s passengers persuaded the captain to let them go ashore to explore a short while. While they were ashore, the winds suddenly returned so furiously that the ship had to sail away, abandoning the nine passengers to their fate.

After a ship had rounded Cape Horn, tension eased noticeably. In only two more months, the ship would reach San Francisco—coasting "downhill" most of the way. That is, unless the unexpected happened.

The Unexpected

At 4:00 on the morning of August 3, the *Andalusia*'s passengers heard a tremendous crash on the deck. The night was clear and the wind had been moving the ship along briskly. Suddenly, the main and mizzen topmasts came crashing down onto the deck.

The passengers rushed out on deck to find chaos. The sails hung in disorder. The decks were littered with ropes and pieces of mast. The ship, still moving forward, rocked from side to side. All the officers and sailors tried to clear away the wreckage and rig up a temporary sail and mast. Only the foresail and the jib were still working. The nearest port was Callao in Peru, nine hundred miles away.

"We can make it," the captain said, "in about three or four

weeks. Unless we have a lee shore and get a bad gale. Then it would be extremely difficult to keep her offshore."

"What alternative have we?" asked a worried passenger.

"We're lucky everything fell on the deck," the captain answered. "We do have enough men and equipment to fix it ourselves."

The crew offered to work day and night. When the passengers also volunteered to help, all on board set up a cheer. The next day, after an early breakfast, the work began. Unfortunately, no one realized it was Sunday.

"All hands were so impatient to get to work," said Ann Booth, "that they did not wait for Mr. Taylor's ceremony, much to the horror of that gentleman. He tried arguing with the captain for desecrating the Lord's Day by working on the mast, but he got a withering rebuke. Poor man, his

Storms were not the only danger at sea, as these survivors from the fire that destroyed the clipper *Hornet* discovered 1,000 miles from land

simplicity amuses me, but it's annoying. No doubt he is perfectly sincere and would practice what he preaches to others, but his fastidiousness never was more out of place than on the present occasion when common sense suggests the necessity of yielding to the emergency."

The men worked as if their very lives depended on it. Those who could not work were busy fetching and carrying ropes, tools, and meals. Delicate hands which looked as if they had never done anything harder than hold a pen were held up proudly to show blisters. Mr. Taylor and his family stayed inside their cabin, since his presence on the deck might appear to lend his sanction to the day's work.

Soon a new mainmast was raised and the ship stopped its continuous rocking from side to side. The sails were bent on the new spars and after a few days of heavy work, the ship was moving on as fast as ever.

The Gate

As the ship neared California, more sails were seen on the horizon. Now every ship they saw was headed for San Francisco. The passengers on one of the ships they spoke said they were carrying the parts of a steamship in the hold. As soon as they landed, the owners (four young men) planned to put their steamship together and make their fortune carrying gold seekers up the Sacramento River to the mines.

Signs that the ship was approaching San Francisco became more obvious. Every portion of the ship was scrubbed and the decks polished with holystones. Woodwork was painted and the sailors hung a sign:

"Please do not spit on the paintwork."

On September 21, just a little over five months after leaving Baltimore, the *Andalusia* was in a thick fog. Everyone knew that fog meant land was near. Dozens of other ships were tacking back and forth in the fog searching for the entrance to the harbor. Suddenly, at 10:00 A.M., the fog lifted. Land was only half a mile away. As the *Andalusia* sailed through "The Gate" (it was not yet called the Golden Gate), the passengers were so moved they could hardly speak.

"I cannot tell my first emotions at this moment," said Ann Booth. "They were so mingled. Joy at having safely arrived —but the predominant feeling is the sad realization of how far I am from home."

Spread out before them was the "city" of San Francisco— made up mostly of tents and campfires. A quick trip ashore —to get their letters being held at the post office—gave the passengers a hint of what was in store for them.

A boardinghouse room cost $50 a week, while the meanest kind of tenement room (made of canvas) cost $300 a month. Two of the men from the *Andalusia* rented rooms for $34,000 a year in a hotel built of canvas. One egg cost one dollar and a suit of clothes $200. The new city did not even have streets. On one road was a sign:

"This street is impassable. Not even jackassable."

The captain of the *Andalusia* had not been to San Francisco since the discovery of gold. He was appalled to learn that most of his sailors intended to get shovels and head for the hills, leaving him to worry about his ship alone. Ann Booth and her husband bought a tiny piece of ground, 25 feet by 60 feet, for $10,000. The captain gave them the mizzen topgallant sail from the *Andalusia* to use as a roof for their new "house."

"When it is painted and stretched over boards," said Ann, "it won't leak in the rain."

Only two years later, the first clipper ship, *The Flying Cloud,* sailed into San Francisco harbor. Her decks were lined with happy passengers. The crew cheered and shouted out what sounded like an unbelievable record.

"We left New York the 3rd of June!" they called out, claiming that theirs was the fastest ship in the world.

"But that's less than three months ago!" shouted the captain of a brig.

"Eighty-nine days and 21½ hours, to be exact," said Captain Josiah Cressy. He did not think it necessary to mention how many spars and masts his crew had mended, but he did tell everyone that in one day of 24 hours, his clipper had made 433 miles. Not even steamships for the next twenty-five years could beat *The Flying Cloud*'s record. Again Americans had found a faster way to take them farther west.

8

By Wind, Water, and Wagon Today

Today's travelers no longer need to join long lines at gasoline stations and drive bumper to bumper along interstate highways on their vacations. They can try a different kind of trip, one that puts them in touch with their pioneer ancestors as they moved westward.

Wilderness Packtrips

Travelers young and old can still follow on horseback many of the same trails that pioneers of long ago used. On a wilderness packtrip, adventurers see breathtaking mountains, miniature valleys in the distance, hidden lakes and waterfalls. They experience views that even a camera with a wide-angle lens cannot record faithfully. They need only to pack their clothing, sleeping bags, and folding fishing pole. For about fifty dollars a day, they join a group of horseback travelers into areas that have never seen a highway. Guides, packers, and cooks go along to make the vacation worry free.

Stagecoach Rides

Some western outfitters still offer stagecoach and wagon rides to those who want to capture more of the pioneer spirit. The travelers pack jeans in a duffle bag and head for prairie land. Each group meets the same conditions that challenged families in the early days—streams to be forded, muddy roads, and even an attack by not-unfriendly Indians. At night, the modern stagecoach traveler stops at an open campfire for a good chuckwagon dinner prepared by an experienced cook, and entertainment under the prairie sky.

Canalboat Rides

Many canals disappeared when the railroads came, but the Erie Canal is still there. Now called the New York State Barge Canal, it can be used by anyone who owns or rents a boat. Canoes, sailboats, powerboats, houseboats, all can travel across New York State to Lake Erie or else go north to Lake Ontario.

At many towns built along the old canals, summer visitors can take day trips on portions of the waterways that are still usable. Some canals provide nighttime trips on which riders can experience some of the thrills that old-time canalboat travelers mentioned in their journals—the incredible beauty of the stars from a dark canal "road" and the oncoming lights of another canalboat. The Chesapeake & Ohio Canal along the Potomac River, the Whitewater Canal in Matamora, Indiana, and the Lehigh Canal at Easton, Pennsylvania, are just a few that provide short rides.

Keelboats and Flatboats

The closest that today's traveler comes to a flatboat or a keelboat is the modern houseboat. With two outboard-inboard engines, houseboats can move either with or against the river current. Just like the earlier boats, houseboats have a living-dining area, kitchens, sundecks, porches, and comfortable beds. Unlike flatboats, they cost about $300 to $500 a week to rent. Everything except gasoline and food is supplied.

Families travel down large rivers today much more safely than their ancestors. They have charts that show the dangerous places. Dams keep huge trees from washing down on the floods to snag boats. Hazards like the Falls of the Ohio were long ago tamed by locks. But traveling on America's rivers still has the same thrills for today's adventurers and many of the same comforts, such as anchoring for the night in a quiet piece of water.

Covered Wagons

Today's covered wagons are mostly recreational vehicles, vans and trailers that burn costly fuel. But it's not too late to take a genuine covered wagon trip that moves slowly back into country where no motor home could possibly go.

One trip in Kansas takes adventurers for a three-day excursion across wilderness country. They ford streams, sleep under the stars, and enjoy campfire cooking. A Wyoming wagon train wanders along unused roads in the foothills of the Rocky Mountains, giving travelers views of the Tetons.

These trips feature Conestoga wagons with a few changes that are most welcome—there are foam-rubber seats instead of hardwood, rubber tires instead of iron, and they are pulled by horses instead of plodding oxen.

For the traveler who seriously wants to know how it was to be a pioneer in a wagon train, there is a trip in North Dakota. Every person wears pioneer and western clothing, meaning long dresses for all the girls and women. Men wear western-style outfits with vests and suspenders. Hats and bonnets are required for protection from the sun. Jeans can be worn by those riding horseback. For swimming, everyone wears cutoffs and sneakers. Travelers in this train take along their musical instruments, their singing voices, craft materials, and nature lore. But they must leave behind their suitcases, transistor radios, iceboxes, coolers, and alcoholic beverages. Everyone helps with the cooking, woodchopping, fire building, water carrying, and cleaning chores.

Under Sail

For the salty feel of sailing in the big old ships, a venturesome traveler can sign on for a one-week to three-week cruise on a windjammer, whaler, or coastal schooner. Prices are reasonable and usually include barbecues on uninhabited islands, a lobster or crab feast, deepwater swimming, snorkeling, and fishing, a chance to climb the rigging or to take a turn at the wheel. They won't be sailing around Cape Horn, because few travelers are fearless enough to try that, but they follow the wind in the calmer waters of bays and along the coast.

To Find Out More

If you want to travel using more of your own energy and less from a machine, here are a few ways to find out more. First, look through your local library under "Travel" and related subjects. Read the travel section of the Sunday newspaper. Many magazines carry advertisements for these unique ways of traveling. Travel agents can often make reservations or supply you with addresses where you can write for more information. Meanwhile, here are a few addresses just to get you started:

Travel by covered wagon, pack train, stagecoach:

FORT SEWARD, INC.
P.O. Box 244
Jamestown, N. Dak. 58401

WAGONS HO, INC.
600 Main Street
Quinter, Kans. 67752

WAGONS WEST
L. D. Frome, Outfitter
Afton, Wyo. 83110

Travel by sailing ship:

MYSTIC WHALER
7 Holmes Street
Mystic, Conn. 06355

THE VICTORY CHIMES
Rockland, Maine 04841

WINDJAMMER "BAREFOOT"
CRUISES," LTD.

P.O. Box 120
Miami Beach, Fla. 33139

Travel by canoe, sailboat, bicycle, snowshoes, skis, kayak, etc.:

COLORADO OUTWARD
BOUND SCHOOL
945 Pennsylvania Street
Denver, Colo. 80203

DARTMOUTH OUTWARD
BOUND CENTER
P.O. Box 50
Hanover, N.H. 03755

HURRICANE ISLAND
OUTWARD BOUND SCHOOL
P.O. Box 429
Rockland, Maine 04841

MINNESOTA OUTWARD
BOUND SCHOOL
308 Walker Avenue South
Wayzata, Minn. 55391

NORTH CAROLINA OUTWARD
BOUND SCHOOL
P.O. Box 817
Morganton, N.C. 28655

OUTWARD BOUND, INC.
384 Field Point Rd.
Greenwich, Conn. 06830

NORTHWEST OUTWARD
BOUND SCHOOL
0110 S.W. Bancroft Street
Portland, Oreg. 97201

SOUTHWEST OUTWARD
BOUND SCHOOL
P.O. Box 2840
Santa Fe, N. Mex. 87501

BIBLIOGRAPHY

Here are some of the books that told me about traveling west in the young United States. Many are so old that only a few copies remain in existence now. They are kept in special historical library collections.

American Journeys, ed. by E. D. Bennett. Travel Vision, a division of General Drafting Company, Inc., Convent Station, N.J., 1975.

Ashe, Thomas, *Travels in America in 1806, Exploring the Mississippi, Allegheny, Monongahela, and Ohio Rivers.* Printed for Richard Phillips, London, 1809.

Baldwin, Leland D., *The Keelboat Age on Western Waters.* University of Pittsburgh Press, 1941.

Banning, Thomas A., *Pioneers, the Narrative of N. H. Letts and Thomas A. Banning,* ed. by Paul M. Angle. The Lakeside Press, R. R. Donnelley & Sons, Co., 1972.

Bannon, John Francis, *History Below the Jet Trails.* American Airlines Historical Series, about 1946.

Beard, James, *James Beard's American Cookery.* Little, Brown & Co., 1972.

Bell, Reverend William, *Hints to Emigrants.* Edinburgh, 1824.

Benson, Adolph B., *Peter Kalm's Travels in North America,* Vols. I and II. Wilson-Erickson, 1937.

Bowles, Samuel, *Our New West.* Hartford Publishing Co., 1869.

Brackenridge, Henri M., *Recollections of Persons and Places in the West.* 1834.

Brennan, John Payne, *20,000 Feet Over History.* American Airlines Historical Series, about 1946.

Brown, Dee, *The Gentle Tamers: Women of the Old Wild West.* Bantam Books, 1974.

Butler, Margaret Manor, *A Pictorial History of the Western Reserve 1796 to 1860.* Published by the Western Reserve Historical Society, Cleveland, Ohio, 1963.

Carey, Mathew, *Carey's American Pocket Atlas,* 3d ed. Philadelphia, 1805.

Carrington, Dorothy, *The Traveler's Eye.* Pilot Press, London, 1947.

Caruso, John Anthony, *The Mississippi Valley Frontier.* Bobbs-Merrill Co., 1966.

Chase, A. W., *Dr. Chase's Recipes or Information for Everybody.* Published by R. A. Beal, Ann Arbor, Mich., 1872.

Clappe, Amelia K., *The Shirley Letters.* San Francisco, 1922.

Cobbett, William, *A Year's Residence in the U.S. of A.* Clayton & Kingsland, New York, 1818.

Cooper, James Fenimore, *Notions of the Americans Picked Up by a Traveling Bachelor.* Carey, Lea & Carey, Philadelphia, 1826.

Cross, Wilbur, and Cross, Farrell, *A Guide to Unusual Vacations.* Hart Publishing Co., 1973.

Dana, Richard Henry, *Two Years Before the Mast.* 1840.

Darby, William, *The Emigrant's Guide to the Western and Southwestern States and Territories.* New York, 1818.

Dickens, Charles, *American Notes.* London, 1842.

———— *The Uncommercial Traveler.* Harper & Brothers, 1860(?).

Dunbar, Seymour, *History of Travel in America.* Bobbs-Merrill Co., 1915.

Earle, Alice Morse, *Stagecoach and Tavern Days.* Macmillan Co., 1900.

Ewan, Joseph and Nesta, *John Lyon, Nurseryman and Plant Hunter and His Journal, 1799–1814.* Published by The American Philosophical Society, Philadelphia, 1963.

Frank Leslie's Illustrated Weekly, newspapers.

Freshfield, Douglas W., and Wharton, Capt. W. J. L., *Hints to Travellers, Scientific and General,* 6th ed. Royal Geographical Society, London, 1889.

Hamilton, Alexander, *Gentleman's Progress: The Itinerarium of Dr. Alexander Hamilton in 1744,* ed. by Carl Bridenbaugh. University of North Carolina Press, 1948.

Hess, Selmar, *All Around the World, An Illustrated Record.* New York, about 1860.

Hungerford, Edward, *Wells Fargo: Advancing the American Frontier.* Random House, 1949.

Inquire Within for Anything You Want to Know. Dick & Fitzgerald, New York, 1856.

Kenny, James, *Journal to Westward, 1758, 1761.*

Ker, Henry, *Travels in the Western Interior, 1808–1816.*

Kitchener, William, *The Traveler's Oracle, or Maxims for Locomotion and Preserving Health.* 1827.

Magoffin, Susan Shelby, *Down the Santa Fe Trail and Into Mexico in 1846–7.* Yale University Press, 1926.

Marcy, Randolph B., *The Prairie Traveler: A Handbook for Overland Expeditions.* Harper & Brothers, 1859.

Martineau, Harriett, *Retrospect of Western Travel.* New York, 1838.

McCullough, Robert, and Leuba, Robert, *The Pennsylvania Main Line Canal.* Morison's Cove Herald, Martinsburg, Pa., 1962.

McRobert, Patrick, *A Tour Through Part of the North Provinces of America: Letters Wrote on the Spot.* Edinburgh, 1776.

Melish, John, *A Geographical Description of the World.* Published by John Melish and Samuel Harrison, 1818.

Meyer, Balthas Henry, *History of Transportation in the U.S. Before 1860.* Peter Smith, 1948, reprinted with permission of Carnegie Institution of Washington.

Michaux, F. A., *Travels to the Westward of the Allegheny Mountains in the States of Ohio, Kentucky, Tennessee and Return to Charleston Through the Upper Carolinas.* 1805.

Moore, S. S., and Jones, T. W., *The Traveller's Directory or A Pocket Companion.* Printed for Mathew Carey, Philadelphia, 1804.

Parkinson, James, *The Experienced Farmer's Tour in America.* 1805.

Parkman, Francis, The Journals of, ed. by Mason Wade. Harper & Brothers, 1947.

Partridge, Eric, *The Macmillan Dictionary of Historical Slang.* Macmillan Co., 1975.

Power, Tyrone, *Impressions of America 1833–35.* Carey, Lea & Blanchard, Philadelphia, 1836.

Reck, Franklin M., *The Romance of American Transportation.* Thomas Y. Crowell Co., 1962.

Roosevelt, Theodore, *The Winning of the West.* G. P. Putnam's Sons, 1908.

Schaun, George and Virginia, *Words and Phrases of Early America.* Greenberry Publications, Annapolis, Md., no date.

Schultz, Christian, *Travels on an Inland Voyage Through New*

York, Pennsylvania, Virginia, Ohio, Kentucky, Tennessee and Through the Territories of Indiana, Louisiana, Mississippi, 1807–8. New York, 1810.

Searight, Thomas B., *The Old Pike: A History of the National Road.* Uniontown, Pa., 1894.

Shank, William H., *The Amazing Pennsylvania Canals.* Published by American Canal and Transportation Center, York, Pa., 1975.

Shaw, Ronald E., *Erie Water West: A History of the Erie Canal.* University of Kentucky Press, 1966.

The Shirley Letters from the California Mines. Alfred A. Knopf, 1949.

Spafford, H. G., *Pocket Guide for Tourists and Travelers Along the Line of the Canals and the Interior Commerce of the State of New York.* T. and J. Swords, New York, 1824.

Stewart, George R., *The California Trail: An Epic with Many Heroes.* McGraw-Hill Book Co., 1969.

Stowe, Harriet Beecher, "The Canal Boat," *Godey's Lady's Book,* Oct. 1841.

Sutcliff, Robert, *Travels in Some Parts of North America, 1804–6.* 1812.

Thomason, Denny R., *Hints to Emigrants or to Those Who May Contemplate Emigrating to the U.S.A.* Isaac Ashmead, printer, Philadelphia, 1848.

The Tourist, or Pocket Manual for Travellers on the Hudson River, Western and Northern Canals, Railroads and Stage Routes, 6th ed. 1839.

The True American. Philadelphia newspaper, 1803.

Twain, Mark, *Roughing It,* Vols. I and II. The American Publishing Co., Harper & Brothers, 1871.

Waggoner, Madeline Sadler, *The Long Haul West: The Great Canal Era, 1817–1850.* G. P. Putnam's Sons, 1958.

Wakefield, Priscilla, *Excursions in North America in 1806.* Darton & Harvey, London, 1806.

White, Llewellyn Brooke, *The Compass Course Is West.* American Airlines Historical Series, about 1946.

—— *Westward High.* American Airlines Historical Series, about 1946.

These are some of the people who actually traveled toward the West and whose experiences are recorded in diaries and journals for us to read today.

Beebe, Lewis, 1835
Benson, John H., 1849
Booth, Anne Willson, 1849
Bowman, James, 1851
Boyd, Joseph, 1808
Breck, Samuel, 1833
Brobson, W.P., 1825
Buffam, Joseph Curtis, 1849
Davidson, William B.,
    1824–25
Dulles, Joseph Heatly,
    1808–10
Edward, Taylor, 1817
Ewing, Dr. John, 1784
Force, John, 1828
Gibbons, James, 1804
Gould, Jane A., 1862
Hall, Maggie, 1853
Haward, Peter, 1827
Hopkins, Gerard, 1803–04
Huidekoper, Harm Jan,
    1828
Hunt, Nancy A., n.d.

Kenny, James, 1750
Lambdin, Lames R.,
    1807–89
Leland, Charles Godfrey,
    1854–55
Lewis, Elisha B., 1849
Morgan, George,1764
Paul, Joeseph, 1815
Richards, Thomas, 1810
Roderfield, Mary C., 1837
Saunders, Mary, 1847
Warner, Mary, 1864
Warner, Mary Eliza, 1864
Williams, Annabel, 1831
Wilson, James A. L., 1856–59
Yates, Thomas, 1850
Unknown English writer, 1794
Unknown flatboat traveler,
    1825–27
Unknown scout,1854
Unknown traveler,1826–27
Unknown traveler, 1836

ABOUT THE AUTHOR

SUZANNE HILTON was born in Pittsburgh, Pennsylvania, but a family pattern of moving often into strange new neighborhoods started an inquisitiveness that has never been curbed. She attended nearly a dozen schools from California to Pennsylvania before attending Pennsylvania College for Women (now Chatham College) in Pittsburgh and graduating from Beaver College in Glenside, Pennsylvania.

During World War II, she used her knowledge of languages as a volunteer in the Foreign Inquiry Department of the American Red Cross. After the war, she married Warren M. Hilton, an industrial and insurance engineer and Lt. Colonel, U.S. Army Reserve. With their son, Bruce, and daughter, Diana, the Hiltons traveled thousands of miles camping and sailing.

A busy free-lance writer, Suzanne Hilton has written nine books, seven of which have been Junior Literary Guild selections. She now lives in Jenkintown, Pennsylvania.

INDEX

189